REWORKING THE WORKPLACE
CONNECTING PEOPLE, PURPOSE AND PLACE

NICOLA GILLEN
RICHARD PICKERING

RIBA Publishing

© Nicola Gillen, 2023

Published by RIBA Publishing, 66 Portland Place, London, W1B 1AD

ISBN 9781 91412 496 9

The rights of Nicola Gillen and Richard Pickering to be identified as the Authors of this Work has been asserted in accordance with the Copyright, Designs and Patents Act 1988 sections 77 and 78.

All rights reserved. No part of this publication may be reproduced, stored in a retrieval system, or transmitted, in any form or by any means, electronic, mechanical, photocopying, recording or otherwise, without prior permission of the copyright owner.

British Library Cataloguing-in-Publication Data
A catalogue record for this book is available from the British Library.

Commissioning Editor: Clare Holloway
Production: Richard Blackburn
Project Manager: Caroline Ellerby Publishing Ltd
Designed and Typeset by Mercer Design, London
Printed and bound by TJ Books Limited, Cornwall
Cover image: John Sturrock

While every effort has been made to check the accuracy and quality of the information given in this publication, neither the Author nor the Publisher accept any responsibility for the subsequent use of this information, for any errors or omissions that it may contain, or for any misunderstandings arising from it.

www.ribapublishing.com

CONTENTS

ACKNOWLEDGEMENTS — iv
AUTHOR BIOGRAPHIES — v
FOREWORD — vii
INTRODUCTION — 1

PART I PEOPLE

1. THE IMPACT OF THE COVID-19 PANDEMIC ON WORK, CULTURE AND COMMUNITY — 7
2. HYBRID WORKING — 21
3. THE IMPACT OF BUILDINGS ON WELL-BEING — 37
4. DELIVERING POSITIVE SOCIAL IMPACT — 55

PART II PURPOSE

5. OPERATIONALISING THE WORKPLACE EXPERIENCE — 75
6. THE VALUE AND PURPOSE OF PLACE — 87
7. EXPERIENCE DESTINATIONS — 99

PART III PLACE

8. EVOLUTION OF CITIES — 119
9. THE PHYSICAL-VIRTUAL INTERFACE — 133
10. ECOSYSTEMS, COMMUNITIES AND PLACEMAKING — 147

CONCLUSION — 173

NOTES — 177
BIBLIOGRAPHY — 180
INDEX — 181
IMAGE CREDITS — 184

Acknowledgements

Creating this book has been a hugely collaborative effort. The research and ideas are the product of many contributions, many hours of discussion and different cultural perspectives.

We would like to sincerely thank our authors, clients, collaborators and colleagues at Cushman & Wakefield, and the industry leaders who generously gave their time and insights. A particular thanks is due to Despina Katsikakis for kindly writing the Foreword as well as her ongoing invaluable counsel to our team.

Nicola Gillen and Richard Pickering are lead authors of this book, and worked in close collaboration with the co-authors: Sophie Schuller, June Koh, Zoe Humphries, Andrew Phipps, Braelyn Hamill, Rachel Casanova and Laura Danzig. Nicola and Richard led the content overall with the co-authors leading or substantially contributing to individual or sometimes several chapters. Sophie Schuller, in particular, contributed extensively across Part I.

Key contributions were made by Aidan Gavin, Aisling Tannam, Antonia Cardone, Bryan Berthold, Linsey Smith, Steven Zatta, Chris Marrable, Colin Macgadie at BDG, Daria Kulikova, Darren Burman, Dimitris Vlachopoulos, Emma Swinnerton, Erin Untereiner, Gerda Stelpstra, Laura Williams, Marc Rohrer, Mike Burton and the team at AECOM, Nicole Kirsten, Rob Harris of Ramidus and Valerie Schumacher.

We are extremely grateful to the individuals and organisations who helped us with case studies; these really bring the book to life. Thank you to BDG Architecture + Design, BVN, CapitaLand, Derwent London, Diageo, Edge, FaulknerBrowns, Fore Partnership, Foster + Partners, Halo Kilmarnock, Heatherwick Studio, Hines, HMRC, HOK, HqO, Huckletree, Jack Hobhouse, Jaego's House and BellCo, Jan Kattein Architects, Maggie's Centre, Matt Biss and Tishman Speyer, McGregor Coxall, Pat Boyle and ESB, Plus X, Related Argent, Salesforce, SDG House, Selfie Factory, Studio Gang, the University of East Anglia, V7, Virgin Money, WilkinsonEyre and WORKac.

A final heartfelt thank you to our editorial team: Fay Sweet (editor), Charlotte-Vonberg Clark, Jenny Jackson, Angelina Moreau and Sonia Khaliq, our commissioning editor Clare Holloway and the team at the RIBA – whose trojan work have made this book possible.

Author biographies

Nicola Gillen

Nicola is an architect, author, practitioner and teacher, specialising in the relationship between design, people, behaviour and the built environment. She is widely recognised across the industry as a leading authority on workplace strategy, design and behaviour-change management. Previous publications include *Future Office* and *ReThink Design Guide: Architecture for a Post-Pandemic World* (RIBA Publishing). She is a visiting lecturer on the Design Masters Course at the IE School of Architecture and Design, Madrid, Spain.

Based in London, Nicola draws on 25 years' experience working with occupiers and developers internationally. She is the EMEA lead for Total Workplace Consulting at Cushman & Wakefield.

Richard Pickering

Richard is a real estate strategist, thought leader and innovator. He is a futurist and keynote speaker on the evolution of real estate and publishes a regular industry blog and podcast on these subjects.

Trained as both a lawyer and a chartered surveyor, Richard's career has focused on urban renewal, economics, regeneration, technology and corporate strategy, in which areas he has advised leading developers, investors and the public sector.

Richard holds the role of Head of Innovation for Cushman & Wakefield in EMEA, where he drives business transformation to align with emerging industry value models.

Sophie Schuller

Sophie leads Cushman & Wakefield's Living Lab, driving scientific research and insights into the future of work and the workplace. She has over 17 years' experience advising clients on all aspects of real estate, facilities management and strategy, including real estate finance, location and portfolio planning and outsourcing. She holds an MBA from London Business School and an MSc in Neuropsychology from King's College London. Sophie is currently studying for her PhD in neuroarchitecture, researching the relationship between office design, cognition and behaviour.

Sophie is a Partner in the Cushman & Wakefield Occupier Strategy team based in Amsterdam, the Netherlands.

June Koh

June has had a diverse and varied career over the last 20 years, working for and with start-ups, multinationals and government bodies across Asia, Europe and America. As a workplace strategist, she is focused on helping clients turn their workplace aspirations into actionable strategies, working at various scales ranging from singular local offices to global guidelines across portfolios.

She holds an MBA from Manchester Business School and a Bachelor of Music from Berklee College of Music. She is currently a partner at Cushman & Wakefield and the EMEA Workplace Strategy lead.

Zoe Humphries

Zoe is an accomplished leader in the field of 'workplace experience', with over 15 years spent working in consultancy, designing and implementing large-scale workplace experience and change projects for leading organisations across the globe.

Zoe joined Cushman & Wakefield in 2022 where her expertise in workplace strategy, design thinking and change management is being applied to evolving workplace experience for the IFM EMEA team. Specific areas of interest include making information and data meaningful through compelling narrative forms and the application of behavioural economics. Zoe is a Partner and leads Workplace Experience for EMEA at Cushman & Wakefield.

Andrew Phipps

Andrew spent 10 years leading a boutique consultancy, undertaking projects that saw him working in over 40 countries across five continents. He also found time to fit in an MBA at Henley Business School before moving to GfK, the global research house. There he led the UK retail business and then recognised the need for, created and filled the role of Global Director of Digital.

Andrew is Cushman & Wakefield's Global Head of Sustainability Thought Leadership. Before this he led the Business Development, Marcomms & Research, EMEA team.

Braelyn Hamill

Braelyn is fascinated by humanity's interactions with the built environment. An architect, interior designer, technologist, strategist and keen observer of the human condition, her focus is on investigating the experience of work at a global scale.

As a Californian transplanted to London, Braelyn attended the Royal College of Art, where her research received the Helen Hamlyn Centre for Design prize for research into redefining office commute experiences through passive regenerative systems focused on user health. Her workplace research continues to focus on sustainable, equitable systems centring female empowerment and the human experience. She is a senior workplace consultant at Cushman & Wakefield.

Rachel Casanova

Rachel is equipped with more than 25 years of diverse industry experience advising companies on how to transform their real estate assets and location strategy to reinforce long-term business strategies and create workplace experiences unique to a company's needs. In a time of new uncertainty about the future of the office, Rachel provides solutions for a range of location, portfolio and workplace solutions. She is a Senior Managing Director of Total Workplace Consulting, based in Cushman & Wakefield's Manhattan office.

Laura Danzig

Laura has significant experience in ESG consultancy, LEED, BREEAM & WELL Certifications, consulting, net-zero resources use strategies, responsible investing strategies and sustainable design consultancy. She brings her experience in structured finance, studies in economics and environmental science and passion for sustainable urban landscapes to achieving her objective of providing clients with sustainable, cutting-edge solutions that benefit their corporation while positively impacting the surrounding environment in the long term.

Laura leads Sustainability Services for Southern Europe and forms part of the EMEA ESG operational committee as well as Cushman & Wakefield's global sustainability task force.

Foreword

The world has changed beyond recognition. Unpredictable and rapid shifts in society, the economy, politics and technology have set a new paradigm for how we work and live, and the real estate industry is finding a new footing.

Making a positive social impact is now high on the agenda for many organisations, as they face the challenge of navigating change, attracting and retaining talent, and delivering ESG targets.

A silver lining to the Covid-19 pandemic is the accelerated transition from regimented work models of the past to a recognition that work is an activity — something we do, rather than a place that we go to. In turn this informs a new role and shape for the physical workplace.

Every organisation is a unique collection of people. When people thrive, organisations thrive, so the future of the workplace must be centred on people. As technology has neutralised distance, the workplace has to work hard to be a destination that pulls people in, engages and inspires them to do their best work.

This book brings together diverse perspectives, experiences and data from expert practitioners. Their expertise is woven together with case studies to illustrate the changing relationship of people and place. Significantly, it also addresses the concept of purpose and the 'why' of work and workplace.

It is no longer enough to carry on thinking the same way about how we design, plan and manage buildings; new ways of working require a new mindset. Practitioners and employers now need to step back, get rid of preconceptions and behaviours, and embrace new skills and experiences. Building a strong culture that encompasses the full ecosystem of physical and virtual places for work will be central to the success of the future workplace. The best workplaces will not only support a sustainable and productive work culture and employee well-being, they will also engage with their surrounding communities in meaningful and impactful ways.

Reading this book, I am inspired by so many organisations reimagining their workplace activities and I remain very optimistic about the future of the office.

Despina Katsikakis

Executive Partner, Global Head of Total Workplace, Cushman & Wakefield

BCO President 2023–4

Introduction

The new workplace is emerging from the most profound disruption since the dawn of the service economy. By accelerating changes that were already under way, the Covid-19 pandemic has rewritten the rule book about how, when, where and even why we work. No longer academic discourse, these questions have become headline news and dinner party conversation topics for workers across the world. As work has become a hybrid blend of in-person and online activities, this book explores the enduring importance of physical place for meaningful human connection, and how this must be refocused in an increasingly virtual world.

Divided into three sections — People, Purpose and Place — the book explores the rapid change that has been wrought on workers, primarily those who are office-based. It identifies the emerging trends in the reconfiguring of work culture and offers insights into innovations and ideas that are starting to inform the workplace of the future.

Each section contains case studies, practitioner guidance and learning points to help drive theory into practical application.

Figure 0.01: Mood-related conferencing rooms at Huckletree White City, London. Using principles of colour theory, these meeting rooms were designed by Studio RHE to generate the associated properties of the themed colour (see chapter 1).

PEOPLE

The first section, **People**, looks at how workers remain the engine of the service economy in the early twenty-first century. Over the past decade, securing the right talent has moved to the top of the corporate agenda, and increasing efforts have been made by large corporations and progressive landlords to use the workplace as a tool to attract and retain a high-performing workforce. Understanding workers' drivers, motivations and the conditions in which they are most successful is paramount. This book considers how the pandemic has given workers a new voice and how they are using it to say what is important to them.

The pandemic induced a permanent shift in and a rebalancing of the ways in which many office-based workers work and perceive work. Expectations have been reframed around the employer/employee covenant and the standard workday has been recalibrated. The shift has also diversified the channels, platforms and mechanisms for producing and delivering work — virtual, physical, asynchronous, synchronous and more.

The impact on workers has been huge, with greater freedom to work from home and avoid the commute, the opportunity to enjoy extra time for building a healthy lifestyle and the ability to choose more flexible working hours to accommodate family life. Within this change come positive results for people and the planet, but some have found it more difficult. For example, those with small living spaces or who are sharing with several other friends or family members can find concentration challenging, and many feel they may miss out on relationship-building and productive chance encounters by not being physically present with colleagues.

Meanwhile, employers grappling with a lack of data are facing decisions about whether to reduce, repurpose or even dispense with their real estate commitments. Can productivity and company culture be maintained in this new model? How can offices be made more attractive and productive places, and how best can employers invest in staff health and well-being? This is a once-in-a-generation opportunity to redefine the social contract between employers and workers, with well-being, productivity and community all hanging in the balance.

PURPOSE

Purpose forms this book's central section, defining the 'why' of work and workplace. As the service economy skews towards creative, inventive and added-value tasks across sectors, employers increasingly rely on the discretionary effort of their workers, rather than treating them as corporate, playbook-following drones. They need people who will go the extra mile in pursuit of intrinsic reward. In a world where the need to be physically proximate is softening, what is the new role of the workplace in driving purpose, well-being and community?

→ Figure 0.02: A central seating area within Maggie's Centre in Leeds, by Heatherwick Studio (see chapter 3)

Much is talked about the employee 'experience', so we set out what this can mean in practice, and how it can be operationalised in the workplace. We also look at how buildings, services and communities will combine to create both purpose and experience for the workforce of the future. When people can work from anywhere, why choose here?

PLACE

The final section is focused on **Place**. Place defines economic value in real estate. Most of the value of any real estate asset can be explained by its distance from somewhere else, be that the city centre, a piece of infrastructure or an amenity. This rests on well-established urban economics and has framed visions of the future of our cities as dense, swarming metropolises. Since trains enabled people to move further out from urban centres, work and its associated daily commute have defined our business districts. However, as technology starts to neutralise distance, new factors come into play that will reshape our cities and facilitate new work ecosystems. The role of the office is shifting from a place where staff are safely accommodated and managed to a place for supporting learning and connection to community. Investors and office occupiers must now consider the broader social value of their workplaces and work activities. This book considers how cities have changed and will change further, the role of technology in liberating work, and how new communities, workplaces and real estate might emerge as working starts to blend with other activities such as retail and leisure.

The book concludes with thoughts on what all of this means for creating successful places to work in the future. The impact of these recent changes on real estate has been immense, with many offices recording all-time low occupancy rates and responding to demands for new interventions such as improved air quality and a wider choice of amenities, locations and work settings. Meanwhile, reduced numbers of regular commuters are challenging the broader city ecosystem, affecting everything from the revenues of public transport services to entire local economies built around the regular footfall of service workers.

There are new and unexpected outcomes too, including a shift in the power balance between employers and employees, raised consciousness about the importance of mental and physical well-being, and growing numbers of employees evaluating their life choices. And yet, despite such fast-track and seismic change, the office remains at the centre of working life for many. Its design and function are evolving to meet new needs, and it stands as a reminder of the enduring importance of physical place and face-to-face connections, uniting people, purpose and place. In the words of Johann Hari, 'Social media can't compensate us psychologically for what we have lost – social life.'[1]

PART I

PEOPLE

The pandemic induced a permanent shift in and a rebalancing of how office-based staff work and perceive work. This is evident in how people prioritise work time and personal time. Expectations have been reframed around the employer/employee covenant and the standard workday has been recalibrated.

CHAPTER 1

The impact of the Covid-19 pandemic on work, culture and community

INTRODUCTION

As the world emerges from its most significant stress test in generations, work begins on understanding the full impact of the Covid-19 pandemic.

Already evident in the workplace is the acceleration of changes that were under way before the pandemic, such as people adopting more flexible working patterns. The impacts of these changes are numerous, for example the reluctance of many employees to undertake the daily commute and the effect on businesses once reliant on the footfall of office workers. There is a raft of new outcomes too, including a shift in the power balance between employers and employees, raised consciousness about the importance of mental and physical well-being, and growing numbers of employees evaluating their life choices. And yet, despite such seismic change, the office remains at the centre of working life for many. Its design and function are evolving to meet new needs, and it stands as a reminder of the enduring importance of physical space and face-to-face connectivity in an increasingly virtual world.

THE CHANGING NATURE OF WORK: WHERE, WHO, WHEN, HOW, WHY AND WHAT?

Many of the dynamics of what is now known as hybrid working were already in place before the pandemic. Remote working across Europe had slowly increased in the decade before Covid-19, although mostly for part-time or self-employed workers. In 2019, 9% of employees worked from home some of the time, up from just over 5% in 2009.[1] Data around numbers of people working from home pre-pandemic is likely to be under-reported, as many did so on an ad-hoc basis and outside of any official reporting. However, it was the enforced, mass, global adoption of these practices, sometimes referred to as 'the great experiment', that permanently accelerated change. Cushman & Wakefield's Experience per Square Foot survey tool (XSF)™, reported in the 2022 'Office of the Future Revisited' report, identified that in 2022 some 60% of European and UK respondents were working mostly from home, with 47% working at home full time.[2] This research predicts that from 2023, 77% of European and UK knowledge workers will be working from home some of the time (42% with a hybrid split between office and home; 35% predominantly from home). Such significant change has led employees to re-evaluate their relationship with work. The so-called 'Covid-decade' is loaded with questions about where we work and who is working, along with when, how and why, thereby redefining 'what is work?'

A greater understanding of the new work paradigm is critical to post-pandemic architecture, urban planning and management of the built environment. Six key areas under consideration feature below:

1 Where we work

One of the most discussed shifts has been the ability to work from a range of locations, not just the traditional office. This change, in part, facilitates greater personal choice and control for employees over their work environment and potentially supports improved well-being. Another effect is the potential loss of organisational control over the work environment, reduced exposure to corporate culture and therefore the need for employers to focus on what will entice employees back together. And while this is happening, other considerations can be embraced, such as where to locate work to reduce the commute, or how can design serve employees who are neurodiverse, hyposensitive or introverted?

2 Who is working?

The ability to work from a personally selected location may make work more accessible to those previously excluded. For example, remote work, without a commute, may present more employment opportunities for people with disabilities. A greater understanding of a broader range of needs remains a significant focus for architects and designers in delivering more inclusive workplace design.

3. When we work

The pandemic has provided an opportunity for employees to challenge and choose when to work. This is particularly appealing to those looking for increased flexibility in working hours. In a 2021 paper, McKinsey highlighted that 63% of employees require a flexible working mode. Working parents largely make up this group. Wider benefits also identified included improved well-being, better work-life balance and positive economic implications.[3] While flexibility may, in part, be delivered through home working, it also requires that the office should accommodate a combination of virtual, hybrid and in-person interactions.

4. How people are working

Emerging work patterns are increasingly virtual and asynchronous, with clear distinctions between the type of work that happens in an office and that completed elsewhere.[4] As the quest for top talent continues, organisations are becoming more open to part-time working, sabbaticals or portfolio careers, providing employees with the opportunity to broaden their experiences and knowledge, the rewards being that these workers demonstrate increased productivity and inspiration. A greater understanding of evolving working patterns may provide opportunities to design environments to suit changing worker profiles.

5. Why people are working

Pandemic lockdowns delivered the rare time and space for people to evaluate their lives. Some enjoyed the solitude and found freedom in a simpler, more local existence; others struggled. The rates of diagnosed mental health issues in the UK rose by 25% between 2020 and 2021. Rates of depression, burnout and anxiety reached endemic levels and continue to climb.[5] Against this backdrop, research and social commentary reinforce a need for increased connection to purpose through work and for an improved work-life balance, and also highlight the environmental cost of contemporary work practices. As a result, the rationale behind why people are working, in addition to earning money, is a critical component to consider when designing the built environment. Organisations that help employees to connect to their purpose and live their values have been shown to not only succeed in securing top talent, but also to increase engagement, innovation and economic gain.

6. What types of work are they doing?

Accelerated by the growing need for virtual technologies, digitalisation is driving change. In a 2021 report, McKinsey estimated that almost a quarter of the workforce will need to change occupations as a result of job replacement through digital technologies.[6] This is supported by a 2018 report from the World Economic Forum which suggests that '133 million new roles may emerge that are more adapted to the new division of labour between humans, machines and algorithms.'[7]

The nature of work is also likely to change, with more hybrid interactions between virtual and in-person teams, along with increasing automation and the need for knowledge workers to achieve higher levels of creativity and collaboration.

Within this new ecosystem, we need to understand the type of work being delivered. The following dimensions of work represent the spectrum of output, and form a central part of work and workplace planning.

DIMENSIONS OF WORK	
In-person	Virtual
Individual	Team
Active	Reflective
Collaboration	Focus
Synchronous	Asynchronous
Extrovert	Introvert
Teaching	Learning
Innovate	Improve
Explicit	Tacit
Hierarchical	Egalitarian
Human	Automation
Work	Rest

Table 1.01: Dimensions of work – the duality of the new work paradigm

The workplace needs to provide spaces that cultivate the best of what humans have to offer rather than just what organisations need from them.

THE CHANGING NATURE OF WORK CULTURE: SIX TRENDS

Global lockdowns, virtual interactions and travel restrictions upended many long-held beliefs and behaviours. While some people have discovered that they no longer want or need to be in an office, others are rejoicing in the chance to be back together. Demographic differences and personal preference have become more visible and organisations are trying to react.

Typically slow to change, organisational culture is defined and maintained by the collective behaviours of employees and other stakeholders. Six impacts reshaping corporate culture are:

1 Hybrid is here to stay

While the initial phases of the pandemic reimagined the new work paradigm as fully remote, hybrid-working models have become the mid-ground. The data shows that the majority of knowledge-based employees want to work from home some of the time, and one- to two days a week in the office is the popular choice.[8]

New skills need to be learnt in creating, managing and fostering relationships online, and conducting meetings in-person and/or virtually. We need to pivot once more to manage the 'some in and some out' reality of the hybrid-work model. Adding further complexity, different demographics and life stages hold different preferences and capabilities for ways of working.

2 The rising power of employees

There is no shortage of research demonstrating a disconnect between organisational leaders and employees. In a 2021 paper, '"Great Attrition" or "Great Attraction"? The Choice is Yours', McKinsey highlighted systemic differences between what employers *think* employees want and what employees *actually* want.[9] This neatly summarises one of the core changes in work culture: just because you lead, doesn't mean you choose.

This dynamic was further visible in data from Cushman & Wakefield's Experience per Square Foot survey tool (XSF)™, where a distinct difference was seen in expected in-office attendance between employees and leaders. The lack of alignment between employees and their organisations was arguably behind 'The Great Resignation'.[10] For those employees who remained, what followed was 'The Great Renegotiation' – a bid to redistribute power back towards the worker.

While twentieth-century work provided organisations with significant power and influence over the career and life choices of their employees, the trend recently has been moving towards worker autonomy, such as the rise of 'job crafting' – where workers proactively customise their jobs. Organisations understand that to establish a successful future culture, they need more systematic employee engagement in decision making.

◂◂ Figure 1.01: The disconnect between employers and employees. Disengagement is driven by undervaluing the employee's need to feel their work has a purpose.

3 Health is central to work and life

From the first days of the pandemic, health concerns climbed the agenda. The news was full of stories about social distancing and what constituted healthy work environments. For wealthy nations, one example of the heightened interest in personal health was illustrated by a 232% revenue growth in Peloton home workout subscriptions in the first quarter of 2020.[11]

In addition to physical well-being, a spotlight was shone on mental health issues too. Despite poor mental health being at high levels before the Covid-19 pandemic, research has confirmed that lockdown further exacerbated the issues, with women and young people most negatively affected.[12] The growing importance of well-being is explored in chapter 3 (pages 39–40).

4 A need for greater representation, diversity, equity and inclusion

There is a growing understanding of how businesses and workplaces do not reflect or embrace the full breadth of contemporary society. In the World Bank's 2020 report on gender-inclusive urban planning, cities including Barcelona, Vienna and Mexico City were highlighted for driving inclusive urbanism by addressing historical social norms that no longer have a role in modern societies.[13] As an example, the open-plan office environment of the past 70 years may have caused concentration issues for some people. There is a rising appreciation of the negative impacts of hyper-stimulating environments on mental health. These dynamics are discussed in more detail in chapter 3 (page 45).

5 Evidence-based insight – a greater need to know 'why' and 'how'

Data-driven and evidenced-based insights have been at the forefront of most industries for years, but the workplace industry has lagged behind. More focus on managing programmes rather than individual projects requires a continuous-improvement mindset, driving the need for measurement and evaluation.[14] As a result, there is an increasing need to adapt to an agile approach to test, learn and iterate within this new work paradigm. In chapter 5 (page 82) we discuss the role of continual measurement in workplace environments.

Against this backdrop, developing technologies and knowledge are fuelling what is understood about the wider world: the environment, neuroscience, psychology and health. As the sophistication and depth of understanding in these fields grows, so does the opportunity for transdisciplinary learning and innovation. It is a culture of analysis and learning that will also drive the new work paradigm.

CASE STUDY 1.1

The Living Lab, Helix, Utrecht

LOCATION: UTRECHT, THE NETHERLANDS

ARCHITECT/INTERIOR DESIGNER: CUSHMAN & WAKEFIELD

COMPLETION: 2022

There is a growing appreciation of the fact that traditional social science models of surveys and interviews provide a limited understanding of what happens at work. It is from this perspective that Cushman & Wakefield, Netherlands designed and created the Living Lab, Utrecht. Designed in close collaboration with Human Resources, this building represents an effective collaboration between employee groups and commercial functional needs.

Led by a dedicated team of researchers, the Living Lab provides an environment for research collaborations between academic, organisational and employee groups. It connects academic research with policy-makers and service-users in a field lab environment.

A mix of quantitative and qualitative research is undertaken by Cushman & Wakefield, partnering with industry experts, policy-makers and academic institutions to create transdisciplinary research groups.

Ongoing research s focused on the following four pillars:

- mental and physical health and vitality
- the design of inclusive environments
- human productivity, performance and connection
- the alignment of the environmental, social and governance (ESG) framework in the workplace.

Figure 1.02: Central collaboration area at The Living Lab, Utrecht

➤ Figure 1.03: Biophilic design. Caged partitioning creates maximum light filtration, visual separation and acoustic protection.

⌄ Figure 1.04: Dome-roofed cubicles create protected environments for communication.

⌃ Figure 1.05: Bold patterns promote alertness, informality and creativity.

13

INDIVIDUALISM	COLLECTIVISM
Focus is on individual contribution and benefits, such as salary, bonus and performance ratings	Focus is on the value of the team, including the well-being and performance of the team as a whole entity
Focus on my needs and wishes	Focus on our needs and desires
Space and privacy are important – private spaces	Space and privacy are not important – shared spaces
Working from home as it suits me	Working from the office as it helps others
Productivity is the primary goal	Strong relationships are the primary goal
Focus on corporate profitability and competitive advantage	Focus on what is best for society and the planet
Short-term focus on what is 'good' now	Long-term focus on what needs to be 'good' forever
Right to choose personally convenient working styles	Focus on what working style works best for the group
Families and communities are not central to commercial success	Families and communities are central to commercial success
Sharing personal thoughts and opinions is accepted and even praised	Focus on maintaining agreeable group dynamics and consensus
Fast paced	Slow paced

↑ Table 1.02: Individualism vs collectivism. Drawn from the work of Professor Hofstede's Cultural Dimensions Theory on achieving a balance between individualistic and community success.[15]

6 **'We' versus 'I'**

Regardless of the wealth of opportunities offered by the change in workplace culture, there is a risk of becoming more individually focused and less collectivist. Selecting where to work to suit their needs is a positive experience for employees, but what happens when someone's else's experience relies on their presence, such as mentorship or another interdependence? One of the main challenges over the coming period will be balancing individual needs and preferences while simultaneously increasing cohesion, equality and togetherness.

WORK COMMUNITIES AND THE IMPACT OF COVID-19

Strong workplace communities are embodied by interactions, physical or virtual, that feel supportive, inspiring and positive; they make people feel they can bring their most authentic selves to work and believe in the work they're doing, leading to more successful careers and fulfilling personal lives.

The value of organisations rests on the strength of employee connections and how effective these networks are at sharing knowledge. It is this flow of information across organisational networks that encapsulates the functional need of office design.

Traditionally, office design has focused on optimising networks required for productivity. However, an increasing body of research highlights networks that exist beyond just production and need to be facilitated.

In her seminal 'Quantum Theory of Trust' hypothesis,[16] Dr Karen Stephenson, a pioneer in network theory, identified the following six networks in the context of work:

1. Work networks
2. Innovation networks
3. Expert knowledge networks
4. Career networks
5. Learning networks
6. Social networks

Previously, these networks would form and be accessed organically, however with less physical contact, greater understanding about what these networks are is critical, and about the technological and spatial characteristics that support their development. Only once we truly understand the ways in which these networks uphold the pillars of work can we ensure that they are provided for and perhaps improved upon.

1. Work networks

With a third of our lives spent at work, it is not surprising that work communities are a critical pillar of the experience. Many work communities serve multiple purposes, such as pseudo-social groups and support networks, which during the lockdown were temporarily inaccessible or at least reduced. What followed was a defining moment of appreciating that those we call 'colleagues' perform a more multifaceted function.

2. Innovation networks

Organisational innovation is characterised as a new method, idea or product, which requires at least two previously unconnected concepts or resources to be aligned to create something novel.[17] Co-working spaces and innovation hubs use the spatial co-location of people with differing backgrounds to foster these new connections. Increasingly, urban developers are incorporating more communal space into multi-tenanted buildings.

Organisational network analytics – the networks formed at work

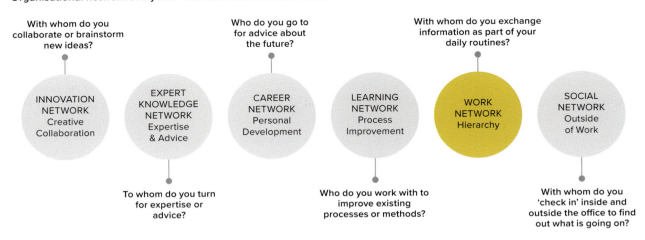

Figure 1.06: The six networks of the work community, based on the work of Dr Karen Stephenson

REWORKING THE WORKPLACE

CASE STUDY 1.02

Huckletree, White City

LOCATION: LONDON, UK

ARCHITECT/DESIGNER: STUDIO RHE

COMPLETION: 2017

Huckletree are providers of co-working spaces. This example in London features a variety of spaces for relaxation and use of colour in meeting rooms to influence mood.

Figure 1.07: The innovative meditation room is designed to evoke relaxation and idea creation.

Figure 1.08 a and b: Mood-related conferencing rooms: using the principles of colour theory, these meeting rooms are designed to generate the associated properties of the themed colour.[18]

3. Expert knowledge networks

Knowledge networks are collections of individuals and teams who come together across organisations to invent and share a body of knowledge. Knowledge can be explicit and tacit, with the latter hard to quantify. Explicit knowledge is believed to account for 10% of all knowledge transfer and includes data, documents, records and files.[19] Tacit knowledge is believed to account for around 90% of information flow and value and is intangible, including experience, thinking, ideas, commitment and competence.[20] It is this tacit knowledge that encapsulates innovation and innovative thinking. Transitioning tacit knowledge to a hybrid work environment is critical for the success of hybrid innovation.

4. Career networks

Career and professional development are characterised by close proximity to mentors and others actively supporting career progression. Research shows that in-person office participation increases the chance of promotion.[21]

Workplace designers should consider the proximity and visibility of key stakeholders, such as mentors, and how space may be designed to create accessibility for those seeking and providing career support. While human resources (HR) programmes and traditional line-management models facilitate some routes to career progression, an increasing trend of retraining and lateral career moves warrants greater connection to a broader range of people.

Traditional hierarchies do not effectively reflect the true communication patterns within organisations. Organisational network maps have been used to quantify the informal network through which information flows. Within these maps, research highlights that natural clusters of employees represent greater network strength than traditional organisational charts. On the basis that organisational network analysis may offer a more accurate representation of the real relationships that exist, this may offer a more effective route for planning employee co-location.

EXPLICIT KNOWLEDGE	VS	TACIT KNOWLEDGE
Explicit knowledge is knowledge that can easily be expressed, communicated and shared	Definition	Tacit knowledge is knowledge that cannot be expressed easily and is often acquired from personal experience
• *Company travel policy* • *Project plan* • *Budget*	*Example*	• *Emotion* • *Innovation* • *Leadership*
Objective, logical and technical	Key characteristics	Subjective, cognitive and experiential
Easily transferable, can be documented and held in documents and database. Can be shared virtually and asynchronously	Ease of transfer	Difficult to transfer, often transferred via social interactions and human connection. Needs to be experienced synchronously
Can be recorded and stored in physical or electronic form	Storage	Cannot be recorded or stored

Table 1.03: Explicit vs tacit knowledge

Formal structure

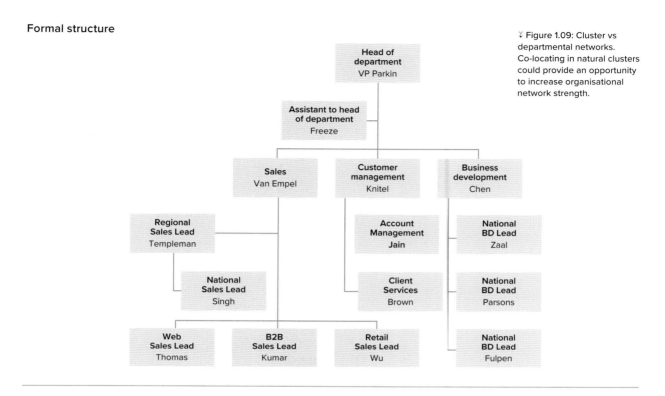

Figure 1.09: Cluster vs departmental networks. Co-locating in natural clusters could provide an opportunity to increase organisational network strength.

Informal structure and clustering

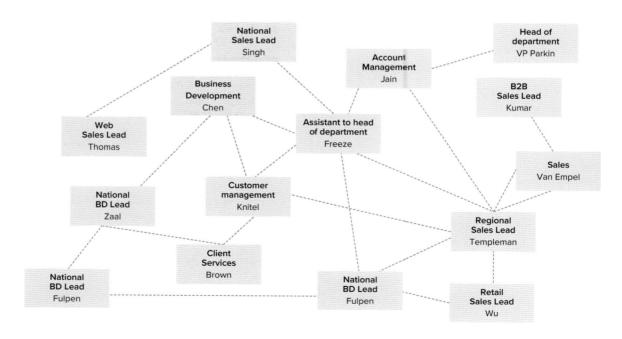

5 Learning networks

The ability to continuously learn and adapt is often cited as one of the most important skills for twenty-first-century work.²² Most cognitive psychologists would agree that learning is an inherently social activity and, as a result, the ability to cultivate adequate learning environments within the workplace is critical.

Successful learning environments typically address the following design issues:

- adequate and healthy environmental qualities, such as natural light, clean air and effective acoustic management
- hypo-stimulating environments for concentration and focus
- hyper-stimulating environments for active collaboration and interactive learning
- adequate space for technology for accessibility and sharing of information
- furniture design to support prolonged periods of reading and listening, including standing desks
- flexible environments to support a broad range of uses such as a theatre, classroom or seminar.

6 Social networks

According to the '2021 Workplace Friendship & Happiness Survey', 57% of people say having a best friend in the workplace makes work more enjoyable, 22% feel more productive with friends, and 21% say friendship makes them more creative.²³ The basis for these effects is evolutionary, with feelings of belonging essential components of 'being part of the tribe'.

However, while the community-building benefits of digitalisation are significant, the story is more complex. Johann Hari, in *Lost Connections,* references John Cacioppo, social neuroscience pioneer, saying, 'we're social creatures. We're meant to be in connection with one another, and when it's mediated by a screen, that's absolutely not there.'²⁴ While this latter point is yet to be substantiated through the field of neuroscience, it highlights the complexity of cultivating social connections in an increasingly hybrid world.

Post-pandemic, organisations are beginning to understand the importance of the workplace as a place to commune, and the value of supporting employees being friends. Encouraging socialisation and bonding is likely to reap economic gains and talent retention.

> **ENVIRONMENTS AND BEHAVIOURAL SETTINGS**
>
> Libraries, churches and hospitals all have a unique ability to elicit the same set of behaviours from a wide range of people. Why? Some psychologists attribute these environmental-behavioural 'rules' to deeply ingrained social norms. However, there is an increasing focus on the role of architecture in cultivating these behaviours called 'psychophysics'.
>
> Psychophysics has been described as 'the scientific study of the relation between stimulus and sensation or behaviour'. And it may lie at the heart of why we all know to whisper in a library and stay silent in a church.
>
> - Objective well-being: Objective well-being is typically aligned with phenomena that can be objectively measured, such as access to shelter, social care, food and education. It is external and can fluctuate with social, political and economic unrest.
> - Subjective well-being: On the other hand, subjective well-being can be less easy to measure as it is largely focused on experience, happiness and purpose. Subjective well-being can be considered an internal process, with some people able to frame challenging life events in a positive way, thus reducing their negative impact.
>
> When health and well-being come together, it can be considered that wellness is achieved.
>
>
>
> Figure 1.10: Huckletree Soho, London. The dreamscape room is designed to transport the inhabitants to a new world, encouraging fresh perspectives.

THE FUTURE DIGITAL COMMUNITY

Communities have been at the heart of the internet and social media platforms since the first days of chat rooms. Fuelled by the rapid adoption of digital communication, digital communities are an increasingly central part of not only our personal lives but of modern-day business.

Digitisation is fuelling the rapid expansion and breadth of organisational networks, as the barriers of time zone, geography and even language are removed. The spatial impact is that, for the first time, workplaces need to accommodate and foster both real-life and virtual communities. This is discussed in further detail in chapter 8.

CONCLUSION

The full impact of the Covid-19 pandemic on work culture, workplace and whole cities is yet to be understood. It is clear that change already under way has been accelerated. In terms of workers – the five-days-a-week commute is dead; more flexible work patterns have been embraced with enthusiasm; the meaning and purpose of work continue to be interrogated; and health and well-being have risen up the agenda. When it comes to physical buildings, debate continues surrounding the workplace function and experience, while, more broadly, city planners, designers and real estate firms are working to address the changing needs in existing and future buildings and districts.

The following chapters set out design and employee behavioural requirements that will need to be addressed for future offices to accommodate and support this radical evolution of work and the workplace.

LEARNING POINTS

WORK:
- The pandemic has had a seismic impact on the power balance between employers and employees, with more choice and control for employees and demands for improved well-being.
- The enforced, mass, global adoption of hybrid-working practices ensures hybrid will stay.
- Distinctions are being generated between the type of work that should happen in an office and that which may be completed elsewhere, or at another time.
- Organisations that support employees to connect to purpose and live their values not only succeed in securing top talent, but also increase the productivity, innovation and economic gain that follow.

- The nature of how and where we work is likely to change, with an increasing focus on hybrid interactions between virtual and in-person teams.
- The office is being seen as the social anchor focused on supporting employees to achieve higher levels of creativity, collaboration and innovation.

CULTURE:
- Building a strong work culture that encompasses the full ecosystem of work is central to the success of the post-pandemic environment.
- The culture of health is growing in importance, with organisations needing to support vitality and positive mental well-being.
- There is also an increasing employee-led drive for sustainability, encouraging organisations and their supply chains to reach carbon neutrality between 2030 and 2050.
- Despite the opportunities this radical change in culture has created, we risk becoming more individually focused and less collectivist.

COMMUNITY:
- The Covid-19 pandemic could be credited with revitalising the concept of community for the twenty-first century.
- Six networks exist and need to be accommodated within a virtual and in-person context of work: work, innovation, expert knowledge, career, learning and social.
- The need to be with each other in person remains as strong as ever, with an increasing focus on architecture and urban planning to create, cultivate and enhance communities.

CHAPTER 2

Hybrid working

INTRODUCTION

In the natural world, the word 'hybrid' is understood as the offspring or product of two species or varieties. This suggests that the phrase 'hybrid working' is a binary concept, choosing between two things — home versus office, physical versus virtual. In practice, hybrid working is far more complex and hinges on the intersectionality of people, organisations, time and place.

The pandemic has not only changed how people work, it has also diversified the channels, platforms and mechanisms for producing and delivering work — virtual, physical, asynchronous, synchronous and so on. So, using the word 'hybrid' is an understatement. The shift has been in progress for some time, but the evolution that occurred during pandemic lockdowns has brought the future of work to the masses — and to the present.

THE REALITIES OF HYBRID WORKING

At the extremes, it might feel that companies are either fully in favour of hybrid working or vehemently against the changes, for example demanding that workers come back to the office. The reality is more complex, full of contradictions and continually evolving. Most organisations are still assessing what hybrid working means for them, but more importantly what the future role of their office is, how to deliver a great employee experience, how best to work in new ways and how to design a future work ecosystem.

Even within organisations, there is variance in how often people want to come back to the office depending on their role — 30% of individual contributors say rarely or never, while 20% of executives/the C-suite say every day or almost every day (see figure 2.01).[1]

The sentiment gap between junior and senior employees is likely to be influenced by the work they perform and their stage in life. Cushman & Wakefield's research shows that executives/C-suite officers reported substantially more positive scores around their hybrid workplace experience, generally feeling greater inspiration, with a stronger sense of belonging and cultural connection.[2] This is not surprising given their position in the company, but also because they are more likely to have additional space in their homes, fewer childcaring responsibilities and so on. In contrast, first-level and senior managers reported low scores when it came to work-life balance and feeling supported by their company. This will have been influenced by their responsibilities at work along with personal commitments and obligations which could include balancing work and childcare.

Meanwhile, the role of the office is becoming clearer — there is strong agreement that it is primarily centred around collaboration, learning and socialising. Since 2020, more of us find it easier to socialise (52%) and collaborate (41%) in the office. We know presenteeism and some management norms still need to catch up (17% cited visibility to leadership as a reason to come into the office); in response, organisations have started providing training for managing remote/hybrid teams.

So, what is keeping workers at home? More than half of people surveyed feel that it is easier to focus, and over 60% feel that it has a positive impact on work-life balance. Access to tools and resources at home have improved too. For a study on what employees want in their workplace, see case study 2.01.

Preferred Office Frequency (Post-Pandemic)	Individual contributor	First-Level Managers	Sr. Managers/ Directors	Executive/ C-Suite
Never/Rarely	30%	14%	5%	17%
1–3 times a month	22%	20%	16%	20%
1–2 days per week	33%	46%	51%	26%
3–4 days per week	11%	13%	26%	17%
Every day or nearly every day	4%	6%	2%	20%

← Figure 2.01: Post-pandemic preferred in-office frequency by seniority, Cushman & Wakefield XSF data, 185,000 respondents, 2020–22

CHAPTER 2: HYBRID WORKING

Metric	Overall	Executive/C-Suite	Senior Managers	First-Level Managers	Individual Contributors
		Deviation from Overall Score (percentage points)			
Inspired	54%	17	2	-2	-1
Belonging	62%	17	5	1	-4
Cultural Connection	56%	18	2	-4	-2
Company Care	53%	18	-1	-4	-1
Renew	47%	15	0	-3	0
Network Activation	66%	11	7	1	-5
Network Strength	66%	12	6	-2	-5
Time for Focused Work	59%	4	-8	-9	4
Company Support of Work-Life Balance	58%	7	-6	-8	2
Work-Life Balance	55%	3	-8	-8	3
Time Away from Work	47%	3	-10	-8	3

Figure 2.02: Variation in sentiments towards work and the office by seniority

Trends for return to office and remoteworking from 2020 to 2022

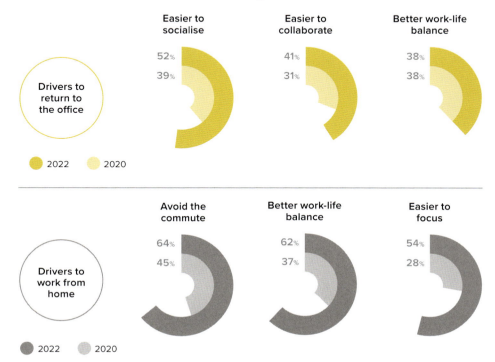

Figure 2.03: Drivers for in-office vs remote working

CASE STUDY 2.01
Experience per Square Foot tool

LOCATION: GLOBAL

CONCEPT: CUSHMAN & WAKEFIELD

To help organisations understand what employees really want in their workplace, Cushman & Wakefield developed the online Experience per Square Foot (XSF)™ tool. The survey poses questions relating to employee preferences, engagement and desired workplace experience. The responses form a database which identifies current trends to inform a better user experience for employees.

Post-pandemic trends indicate that the office and its purpose have shifted, with an increased number of employees finding little or no benefit in attending the office. Employees who do come in say the main reasons are for socialising and collaborating.

There is a clear message about providing employees with the choice of when and where to work to positively increase workplace experience. With companies often focusing more on the 'where', the data show that focusing on the 'when' and providing employees with schedule flexibility can provide a better overall workplace experience outcome (see figure 2.05).

Considering well-being in the workplace, the data collected show that the top four drivers are feeling inspired, feeling energised, being able to achieve a work-life balance and being able to focus at work. When looking at employees with high and low levels of well-being, there is a clear difference in their current workplace experience (see figure 2.06).

What do you like most about working in an office environment?	% of Respondents 2020	% of Respondents 2022	Percentage Point Change
Easier to socialise with coworkers	39%	52%	+13
Easier collaboration	31%	41%	+10
There are no benefits to working in an office	5%	15%	+10
Visibility to leadership	11%	17%	+6
Encourages healthier behaviours	6%	8%	+2
Other	3%	5%	+2
More connected to leadership	11%	12%	+1
More connected to the company culture	16%	18%	+1
I like the commute	3%	4%	+1
More in tune with what's happening in the business	21%	22%	+1
Access to natural light and outdoor space	4%	4%	+1
I feel safer	2%	2%	0
Better work-life balance	38%	38%	0
Helps me be innovative / creative	7%	6%	-1
Helps me stay motivated	13%	11%	-2
I prefer a business environment	9%	6%	-3
Easier to learn and develop	11%	8%	-3
Easier to manage my team	13%	9%	-4
Better technology	13%	8%	-5
Easier to focus	14%	9%	-5
Better workspace setup	22%	15%	-7
Better access to tools and physical resources	31%	21%	-10

« Figure 2.04: Factors driving the return to the office – insights from Cushman & Wakefield's XSF Survey Data

CHAPTER 2: HYBRID WORKING

Employee flexibility to choose where, and especially when, to work drives great experiences
Employees with choice & control over where or when they work report better experiences than those without choice, but choice in work schedule leads to the best outcomes

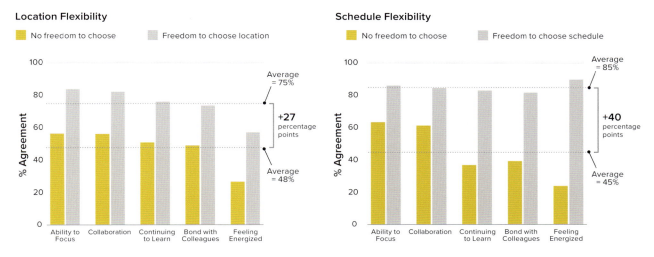

Figure 2.05: The impact of providing freedom to choose where and when we work

Better workplace experiences = higher levels of well-being

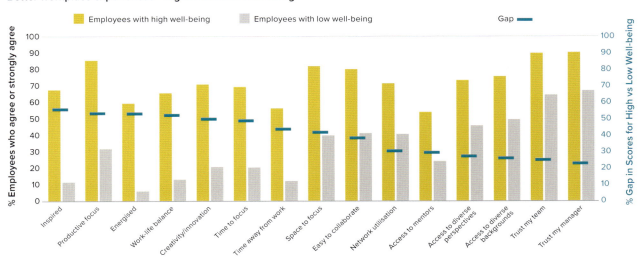

Figure 2.06: The impact of well-being on productivity and experience

25

Figure 2.07: Gap between Millennials' and Generation Z's experience vs all employees by in-office frequency

These trends show the importance organisations should be placing on considering whether and how their workplace strategies support the various activities that benefit well-being.

For younger employees, coming into the office three or four times a week (see figure 2.07) seems to produce the best learning and workplace experience, but this dips significantly when increased to every day or nearly every day. This tells us that while in-person interaction is critical for this group, having the flexibility to work from home is also equally important.

THE CHALLENGES OF HYBRID WORKING

As the workplace and culture evolve, there remain concerns for some. Cushman & Wakefield's research with 300 business leaders across the UK and Europe found they faced challenges including how to define a clear and compelling role for the office and how to develop talent.

Most organisations feel that the role and purpose of the office today, and in the future, is around the following:

- connection, collaboration and creating a sense of community
- facilitating learning, especially informally or through osmosis
- talent attraction and retention
- showcasing the organisational brand, purpose and values

However, office occupancy across the UK barely hit 30% during 2021 and 2022 (see figure 2.08). Regardless of industry sector, Cushman & Wakefield's research indicates that 44% of employees want to go to the office only occasionally and 15% see no benefit in going in at all. This means that organisations must intentionally consider how all the above can also be facilitated virtually, remotely and across an ecosystem of places.

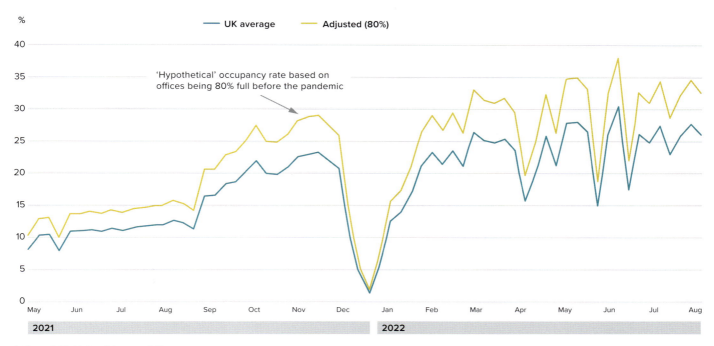

Figure 2.08: National Average Office Occupancy (sample comprising 155 office buildings across 10 major UK cities, covering over 1,500 leases)

HOW HYBRID WORKING MIGHT EVOLVE

While hybrid working continues to mature, a workable definition could be this: hybrid working is having the choice and an enabling infrastructure to work effectively from a variety of places, amidst a culture that drives an equitable work experience regardless of where workers are.

There are broadly three models of hybrid working, and often in larger companies all three might be adopted by different parts of the business.

Hybrid working models

1 Remote working revolving around the office

This first model is where many organisations feel most comfortable. Yes, most employees work from home on a Monday or a Friday, but the expectation is that all the good and important 'stuff' still happens in the office — the town halls, leadership meetings, the free breakfast and so on. The office remains as the headquarters, a mothership.

2 Truly distributed working

In this model, every type of place within the hybrid ecosystem has an equal role. Regardless of where a person is working from, the expectation is that they will have an equitable experience and investment decisions tend to be more balanced across the property portfolio.

3 Remote-first working

There is no traditional 'office' in the mix; employees work remotely all the time or might occasionally drop in at a co-working space. This means that all the infrastructure of process, culture and so on has been built with that in mind.

There is no better or worse model, only one that works for the organisation or the teams within it. And as workers get more comfortable with and adapt to hybrid working, it will continue to evolve. At the end of the first year of the pandemic, many organisations were still unsure about whether hybrid working was here to stay and were cautious about making longer-term investments and decisions to embrace the change. Since then, there has been growing acceptance of the benefits of hybrid team-working.

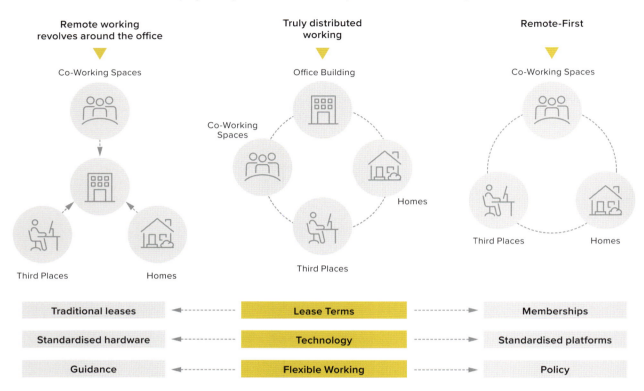

↑ Figure 2.09: Hybrid working models

Data from management consultant Gartner show that for the knowledge-worker population, hybrid working is a good fit.[3] Benefits include the following:

- **Hybrid teams show greater agility:** 70% of hybrid employees agreed that they adapt the structure of their meetings based on the intended outcome against only 49% of on-site employees.

- **Hybrid teams show greater psychological safety:** 66% of hybrid employees reported feeling comfortable taking risks in their role, compared to 47% of their on-site counterparts.

- **Hybrid teams show greater equity:** 69% of hybrid employees reported that their teammates accommodate their working preferences, compared to 54% of on-site employees.

Given that talent attraction and retention is one of the top priorities (if not *the top*) for many organisations, having a considered and cohesive hybrid-working strategy is critical for employee experience and engagement.

THE WORKER RELATIONSHIP WITH DIGITAL ENVIRONMENTS

In this period of rapid change and global uncertainty, it is important to look at the landscape of technology from a holistic perspective, whereby people, place, process and technology are considered together. For an example of technology being used to improve the workplace experience, see case study 2.02.

The spotlight has shifted from technology which enables peripheral connections to digital tools that allow us to experience connection more effectively, interacting in both virtual and physical environments. The evolution of how we use technology to interact, connect and collaborate with colleagues and clients can be broadly defined in the following terms:

Figure 2.10: Worker relationship with digital environments: before, during and after the pandemic. See chapter 9 for more on the physical and digital interface.

PRE-PANDEMIC	PANDEMIC	NEAR FUTURE
SEPARATE AND OBSERVING Conference Calls	**CONNECTED AND SEMI-IMMERSED** Microsoft Teams + VC	**FULLY IMMERSED** VR + Metaverse
• Connection was an active choice. • Focused on talking about what is going to be done and doing it later alone or when all participants can come together in person.	• Immediate connection and availability is an assumption. • Real-time, cloud-hosted documents mean teams are actively working together across platforms while on calls. • Asynchronous collaboration enables work to happen at any time 24/7.	• Protocols and understanding of the toll 'always on' working takes on employees will have matured, to enable more personal control over when and how someone is available for synchronous work. • More agnostic and autonomous working. Connecting when, where and how employees work without missing out on workplace culture or experience.

CASE STUDY 2.02
Property Technology

LOCATION: GLOBAL

DESIGNERS: spaceOS AND HqO

There's been an emphasis on using technology to improve the work and workplace experience by incorporating a new user-centric approach. The goal is to create better tenant-engagement experiences by exploring the whole workday, from the early morning commute to playing sports in the park after work. By collecting meaningful data and providing useful insights, PropTech companies such as spaceOS and HqO aim to bridge the gap between the physical office and the digital workplace by delivering better employee engagement experience.

SpaceOS uses employee engagement platforms to bring real-time energy consumption and carbon-footprint data to its tenants. This enables tenants to better understand and track their energy consumption. Providing employees with this information in a gamified way can also promote positive behaviour change, helping companies reach sustainability goals.

These tenant-engagement platforms also act as a remote control for employees to have access to every aspect of the physical and digital workplace. For example, HqO provides employees with access to office insight data such as office and parking capacity, booking systems to reserve parking spaces, desks or meeting rooms, and access to on-site services, enabling them to best plan their day and take advantage of insights for optimised productivity.

In June 2022, HqO acquired the global workplace employee experience leader Leesman. Having adapted its surveying tool during the Covid-19 pandemic, the Leesman Office Survey contains responses from almost one million office employees and 300,000 home-based employees.

With more employees working from home, retaining a sense of community within companies can be a challenge. However, taking advantage of live-data insights can facilitate employees' day-to-day work routine and reduce any negative barriers associated with coming into the office.

HYBRID WORKING: DIVERSITY AND INCLUSION

Equity in the workplace means giving everyone what they need to perform at their best. Equity is key because it is a mechanism to ensure inclusion. There is little point in building a diverse workforce and then not helping people to succeed.

An example of equity can be as simple as thinking more broadly about technology provision – a salesperson might find a lightweight laptop best suited to their job, but a graphic designer would find that same laptop useless for image rendering that requires more processing power.

Equity can also be realised through behaviours and socialised etiquette around how to behave in a hybrid-working environment. For example, below is an example of Cushman & Wakefield's hybrid meeting principles, which aim to enable all attendees to fully participate in events regardless of how they connect.

The impact of hybrid working on inclusion becomes more nuanced and complex when considering whether or not it levels the playing field. The office is traditionally where employees experience and observe the behaviours and norms that shape culture. In interviews, one senior leader in a top consulting firm said that new recruits from 2020 and 2021, when the pandemic kept people away from offices, had a perception of the work culture as more hierarchical and formal than it really was. They lacked the experience of walking around the office, meeting senior leaders, or having informal chats in the kitchen, and more importantly they had not seen how the rest of the organisation interacted with these senior people.

HYBRID MEETING PRINCIPLES FOR AN EQUITABLE EXPERIENCE

The following hybrid meeting principles provide helpful tips for participants to make the event inclusive for all, whether in-house or working remotely, and to minimise distractions.

Meeting facilitator: The designated facilitator will ensure that remote and in-office participants have an equal experience.

HYBRID MEETING PRINCIPLE	IF YOU ARE IN THE ROOM	IF YOU ARE ONLINE
Should I send a virtual meeting link to all participants?	YES This creates a more equitable environment and makes it easier for remote colleagues to see who is talking.	YES
Should I log into the virtual meeting and have my laptop video on?	YES Try to talk 'to camera' as well as to those in the room and avoid impromptu side conversations.	YES Act like you're in the room. It can be tempting to get distracted and multitask, but people are quick to pick up on this and can disengage.
How do I ask a question?	Use the raised hand symbol in the chat box and then state your question. The meeting facilitator will type the question in the chat box for the online participants.	Use the raised hand symbol and then type in the chat box. The meeting facilitator will read out your question.
How do I make the meeting inclusive for all participants?	Avoid prioritising those in the room. If you see someone unmuting themselves, it is usually a sign they want to speak; try to keep an eye on cues like this.	
How can I ensure good sound quality for all participants?	Please mute the sound on your laptop BEFORE logging in. Stay muted throughout the session.	You may wish to use a headset during the meeting to maintain audio quality when you speak.

Table 2.01: A practical guide to a successful hybrid meeting

Delivering an equitable experience

Hybrid working, when done right, can level the playing field for dispersed teams and remote workers, and support them to do their best work without the fear of being 'passed over' for promotions or career opportunities. For many, the rise of online tools such as Teams and Slack, coupled with behavioural change, has improved access to leadership, management and colleagues.

However, if an organisation's mindset is still very much stuck in pre-pandemic terms, then there is a risk of 'presence privilege' – where only people physically present in offices are visible to management and leadership, or where people working remotely miss out on the social connections that happen only in the office, for example the after-event discussions that happen after a staff all-hands meeting.

To deliver a truly equitable experience, the workplace ecosystem (the tech, the spaces, the policies, the culture, the management systems and so on) needs to be considered holistically.

There is no doubt that hybrid working has good levels of engagement from minority groups, who have shown a strong preference for it. Research from McKinsey has identified the impact of hybrid-working models on diversity, equity and inclusion (DE&I).[4] Its study showed:

- Some traditionally underrepresented groups demonstrated a stronger preference for hybrid working than their colleagues.
- Employees with disabilities were 11% more likely to prefer a hybrid work model.
- More than 70% of men and women expressed strong preferences for hybrid work, but non-binary employees were 14% more likely to prefer it.
- LGBTQ+ employees were 13% more likely to prefer hybrid work than other groups.

How organisations design their future of work will play a part in furthering their DE&I ambitions. While hybrid working is still evolving, one thing is clear – the workplace is, and will continue to be, more people-centric than ever before.

HOW CAN EMPLOYERS MAKE HYBRID WORKING SUCCESSFUL?

The changing nature of work culture (see chapter 1, pages 10–14) means that an organisation's hybrid-working strategy must address more than how much space people need or how many days in the office are required. Giving employees choice, supporting their well-being, creating inclusive environments and building communities must be the core considerations of any hybrid-working strategy. Looking across a selection of over 40 workplace projects in the UK and Europe during 2020 and 2021, figure 2.11 shows what organisations consider to be the purpose of their office.[5]

An innovative 'success-from-anywhere' approach to flexible hybrid working has been created by Salesforce – see case study 2.03.

Our clients' business vision – the purpose of the office
Companies are redefining the purpose of the office to coming together to socialise and connect. These findings were gathered from leadership visioning and business objectives.

« Figure 2.11: Redefining the purpose of the office: insights from Cushman & Wakefield projects 2020–22

CASE STUDY 2.03

Salesforce 'Async Week'

LOCATION: GLOBAL

Known for trialling innovative ways of working, Salesforce introduced a 'success-from-anywhere' model in 2021 – displaying their commitment to a truly flexible form of hybrid working. As part of this, Salesforce undertook a bold experiment to uncover better ways to work and empower employees to manage their time in a way that worked best for them. Dubbed 'async week', tens of thousands of employees tried to go meeting-free for a full week. All employees, regardless of role or seniority, were encouraged to cancel all meetings.

It is hard to change ingrained work habits and pivot out of a meeting culture, but Salesforce has found 'async weeks' to be most successful when:

- People are prepped and given tips, tools and resources prior to the week (e.g. preparation guide, tips for using digital channels, FAQs, etc).
- They are conducted at a sizeable scale; buy-in is required at the team or department level (they've had 23,000 participants in a single week).
- Teams set internal perimeters and expectations around engaging with others.
- Employees are aware of the full range of collaboration tools on offer to them.

'Async week' was positively received by employees, who valued having more autonomy in how to spend their working day; 70% reported feeling less stressed and productivity levels were 72% higher than in the average week. Since the first trial, 'async week' has been adopted more broadly within Salesforce, with some teams choosing to strategically plan them on a quarterly basis ahead of product launches – when focused work is most needed.

In the context of the pandemic, which has created a work culture where we are overly reliant on meetings, 'async week' has not only helped employees to consider when a meeting should and could be replaced by other means (email, Slack clips, etc) but also how to have more effective meetings when you do have them and to be more intentional when communicating.

> It's an exciting time with the evolution of work and a "success from anywhere" approach – but no one has all the answers. We've found that by being experimental and innovative, we will discover what works best for our business and our people.

LISA MARSHALL,
SVP INNOVATION AND LEARNING, SALESFORCE

WHAT DOES HYBRID WORKING MEAN FOR THE OFFICE?

As a result of increased hybrid working, most tenants are looking to reduce their real estate footprint (78%). And space is being used in new ways – often more than half of the office footprint is now used for collaboration, social and well-being spaces (see figure 2.12). Not surprising, given that results from Cushman & Wakefield's Experience per Square Foot (XSF)™ tool has shown that employees who report high levels of well-being are 2.5 times more likely to say they can do their best work compared to their peers with low well-being.[6]

The shift in space allocation is also reflected in the fact that the density per occupant (person in the building) now ranges from about 8.5 to 23 square metres, with an average of 15.7 square metres. This means that although organisations have reduced their overall footprint to account for employees being in the office less than before the pandemic (2.8 days on average post-pandemic), the amount of space per person when in the office still reflects a good-quality experience with access to collaboration, social and well-being spaces.

CHAPTER 2: HYBRID WORKING

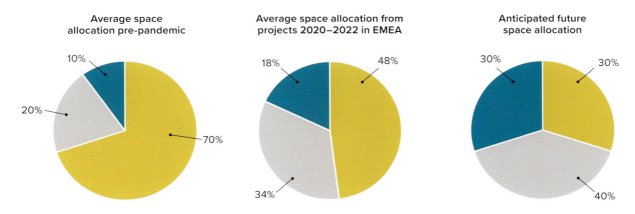

↑ Figure 2.12: The changing allocation of space within the office

HOW TO DELIVER HYBRID WORKING

Looking beyond the office space, organisations need to explore how to evolve a workplace experience and decide how the integral parts of a hybrid experience — human resources (HR), IT and real estate (RE) — work together to deliver this.

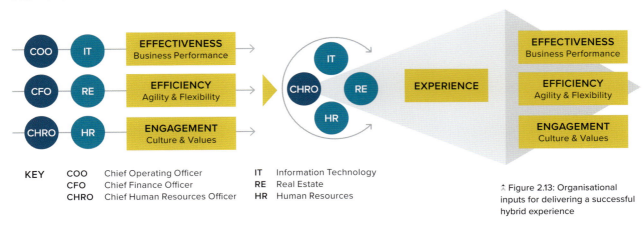

↑ Figure 2.13: Organisational inputs for delivering a successful hybrid experience

33

The first step to successful hybrid working is to consider all the components within the hybrid ecosystem, as follows:

ENABLERS

Leadership – senior sponsorship who truly believe in the workplace vision

Culture – behaviours needing to change or keep to support hybrid working

Policy – guidance and policies to support hybrid working

Technology – the right technology strategy to support in-person, remote and hybrid working

CURATORS

Human touchpoints – the day-to-day interactions of employees, everything from events, meetings, arrival, logging onto laptops at home and so on

Integrated delivery team – aligning HR, IT and RE teams from vision through to implementation

PLATFORMS

Ecosystem of places – the variety and scope of physical places to suit the various activities and needs of employees

Technology – applications and interfaces, and how well they integrate remote, in-office and hybrid working/collaboration.

HYBRID WORKING AND THE IMPACT ON NEIGHBOURHOODS

Working in an office has shaped so much more than the buildings themselves. For example, take the 1.3 million private-sector office workers in New York City; before the pandemic, a typical NYC worker would spend around $13,700 a year near their office. As a result of hybrid working, the typical NYC worker is projected to spend $6,730 less.[7] This means almost $9 billion a year less going into the local economy in total — and considerable potential changes to small businesses and the retail/F&B/entertainment landscape.

Transport for London (TfL) reported that ridership since January 2022 regularly reached only around 60% of pre-pandemic levels, while weekend ridership has gone up to about 75% of pre-pandemic levels.[8] All of this points to an excess of space left in cities.

It takes an ecosystem of partners to deliver a great experience

Workplace and people experience

↑ Figure 2.14: Components of a hybrid ecosystem

CO-WORKING RISES TO THE CHALLENGE

While many occupiers are slow to repurpose their assets, co-working spaces have been quick to respond to the changes brought on by the pandemic and hybrid working. When asked, during the middle of 2021, nearly two-thirds of tenants indicated they were using and/or planning to grow their use of flexible office space.[9] And while many workers noted the benefits of home working, the second most common complaint was having 'no divide between work and home life'. Flexible offices can act as third places closer to where people live. While well-known workspace brands such as WeWork primarily still focus on city-centre locations, it is now more common to see smaller, community-based co-working spaces on the ground floor of new-build apartments and around residential neighbourhoods. Having people spend more of their week at or closer to home contributes to local economies. See chapter 8 for how this change is shaping the evolving city.

CONCLUSION

Hybrid working is here to stay. It is the first time that most employees have been able to take control of their work and time, and they won't give up these freedoms easily. The model will evolve over time.

LEARNING POINTS

- Hybrid working is not a binary concept and reflects the wider shifts in how work and workers have changed.
- Hybrid working is still evolving and there is no one-size-fits-all model, nor one right answer.
- There is a wide variance in the preference for hybrid working depending on role and demographics.
- The sentiment gap between junior and senior employees is wide, with executives and the C-suite reporting substantially higher scores around workplace experience.

- The role of the office is becoming clearer and is centred around connection, collaboration and socialising.
- A better work-life balance is a key reason for preferring to work from home. Over 60% of workers feel that it has a positive impact on their work-life balance.
- Delivering a successful hybrid-working strategy requires organisations to consider all the components within the ecosystem, and an integrated delivery team consisting of at least HR, IT and RE.

- Equity in a hybrid-working environment is critical to ensure that organisations enable all their employees to perform at their best regardless of where they work.
- The office is traditionally where employees pick up cultural norms; how do we ensure culture is not eroded as we spend less time in the physical office together?
- Giving employees choice, supporting their well-being, creating inclusive environments and building communities must be the core considerations of any hybrid-working strategy.

CHAPTER 3

The impact of buildings on well-being

INTRODUCTION

The workplace is becoming better understood as a place to actively and holistically impact health. Greater emphasis is being placed on human-centric design to create environments that cultivate positive, happy and enjoyable experiences, which ultimately inform positive health and well-being outcomes.

This design focus is further fuelled by advances in transdisciplinary areas such as neuroscience and psychology. To successfully design buildings that facilitate and nurture humans, a greater understanding is required of what it means to be human. This chapter explores the basis of being human at work and the dimensions of well-being to be cultivated and nurtured within office design.

WHAT DOES IT MEAN TO BE HUMAN?

Before we can design a workplace to address the full needs of employees and foster health and well-being, we must first understand what it means to be human, to determine who and what, exactly, we are designing for.

In his eponymous pyramid-style structure, psychologist Abraham Maslow identified seven categories of human needs that ultimately influence and dictate all behaviour and inform well-being. Maslow suggested that needs should be met in inverse order; basic biological and physiological needs are to be dealt with before an individual can focus on or achieve motivation to tackle the secondary or higher-level needs.

For office environments to support the basis of what it means to be human and, as a human, to achieve states of health and well-being, designers and architects need to understand and cater to these needs. Figure 3.01 is a spatial translation of Maslow's 'Hierarchy of Needs', highlighting the specific work and workplace-related interventions required to meet an employee's needs, leading to self-actualisation,[1] which is associated with well-being.

➤ Figure 3.01: Maslow's Hierarchy of Needs — a spatial translation. Once employees' needs are met through adequate workplace design and organisational support, a more systematic approach to well-being can be pursued.

SELF ACTUALISATION
Reaching one's potential; living in alignment with values and purpose; accomplishment; state of flow; spiritual alignment; achieving desired states of parenting, relationships, career success, utilisations of talents and abilities

AESTHETIC AND BEAUTY
Beauty can be found in a combination of: Shape; Colour; Sound; Touch; Smell; Temperature; Light; Form; Other psychological and physiological sensations; Spaces that feel secret and special

COGNITIVE
Spaces to inspire and engage the mind: learning; knowledge; creativity; curiosity; purpose. *Spaces to relax the mind:* cognition-free spaces; no-tech zones; relaxing environments; meditation pods

ESTEEM
Accommodation of external esteem: Appreciation boards, visibility of performance and group achievement. Facilitation of internal esteem and cultivation of self-respect; perseverance; resilience; competence; selfconfidence; independence; freedom

BELONGING AND LOVE
Feeling part of the team; consideration on team-days for hybrid-working environments; cultivation of trust, inclusivity, family, friendship, intimacy, acceptance, the giving and receiving of affection, tribing

SAFETY
Physical security — Accessibility, mobility and security; Financial security — Effective policies to protect job and financial safety; Personal security — Spaces to retreat and hide when not feeling safe; Emotional security — Avoid space composition that suggests being 'watched' by management

BIOLOGICAL AND PHYSICAL
High-quality environments (air, light, sound, temperature); Provision of different types of bodies (gender, gender neutral, acute and chronic conditions, such as pregnancy and menopause); Access to hygienic toilets and sanitary provisions; Access to nutritional food, water and refreshments; Space for sleep, rest and relaxation (often overlooked within the modern context of work)

THE EIGHT DIMENSIONS OF WELLNESS

As discussed in chapter 1 (page 11), the pandemic has recontextualised our relationship with health and well-being and nowhere more importantly than in the office. Previously seen as a personal responsibility, there is an increasing focus on the role of organisations and workplaces in facilitating healthy environments and evaluating whether work practices are causing poor health.

While the correlations between poor physical health and the built environment have been well documented through phenomena such as sick building syndrome, mental health is one area of growing concern.[2] The UK Household Longitudinal Study (UKHLS), tracking levels of psychological distress among adults aged 18 and over,

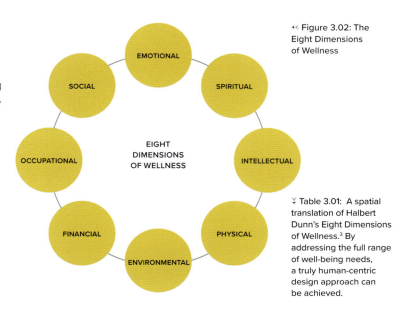

Figure 3.02: The Eight Dimensions of Wellness

Table 3.01: A spatial translation of Halbert Dunn's Eight Dimensions of Wellness.[3] By addressing the full range of well-being needs, a truly human-centric design approach can be achieved.

WORKPLACE CONSIDERATIONS FOR DIMENSIONS OF WELL-BEING

Physical
- stand-up, sit-down desks
- ergonomic design throughout the space
- design for movement, moving between spaces to suit different activities, i.e. strategic positioning of coffee points, meeting rooms to encourage variety and avoid zoned 'command centres'
- access to space for physical activity
- consideration of office design for a range of body types, genders, ages, demographics and physical abilities
- healthy and nutritional food, access to water
- ability to rest, de-stress and engage in leisure activities
- prevention of injury and illness, and management of chronic health conditions

Environmental
- outside access to green spaces
- biophilia throughout interior design
- high-quality environments (air, light, sound, temperature)
- minimising destruction and degradation of the outside environment (including energy consumption, commuting and meat consumption)

Financial
- affordable services, including access to food and beverages
- strong policies to provide job and financial security
- access to employment-related services, i.e. healthcare, counselling, training

Occupational
- visibility of and access to equal, equitable and inclusive career and development opportunities
- learning and development
- ability to effectively balance work with other aspects of life
- consideration of specific occupational health groups, e.g. women (support for breastfeeding, menstruation, menopause)

Social
- ability to make and maintain friendships
- space and time available to bond
- representation and inclusion of diverse individuals and groups (DE&I)
- support and connectivity to local communities, e.g. charity days and supporting local business through pop-up stalls
- fostering citizenship
- opportunities to give and receive feedback

Emotional
- cultivate proximity to purpose and joy throughout the workplace
- create spaces that support inclusive and supportive leadership philosophies
- provide diversity in design from busy, interactive spaces to quiet, isolated spaces
- provision of space to hide, cool-off, decompress, rest, focus, be uninterrupted
- design mind-friendly environments with service users and diverse groups

Spiritual
- space that supports living in accordance with the values of employees
- cultivation of living with purpose
- inclusive workplace services that reflect the religious and spiritual beliefs of employees
- provision of faith and spiritual rooms

Intellectual
- space to support creativity, innovation, learning, problem solving, analytics, concentration and comprehension
- space to spark curiosity, sharing of knowledge and self-improvement
- new and exciting experiences/services or spaces that introduce 'delight'
- cultural, community involvement
- proximity to learning

> **ARE HEALTH AND WELL-BEING THE SAME?**
>
> While the words 'health' and 'well-being' are sometimes seen as interchangeable, there are clear distinctions which have a differing impact on the design process.
>
> The World Health Organization defines health as 'a state of complete physical, mental and social well-being, and not merely the absence of disease or infirmity'.[7]
>
> However, definitions for well-being are slightly less clearly defined. The Oxford English Dictionary defines well-being as 'the state of being comfortable, healthy, or happy'.[8] Wider definitions used within academic literature highlight well-being as a process to achieve health, and highlight that while health and well-being inform one another, they are not mutually exclusive; one can be in good health but have poor well-being and vice versa.
>
> Further complexity lies in the fact that well-being can be subjective and mean something different to different people. However, researchers agree that well-being holds a subjective and objective dimension.[9]
>
> - Objective well-being: Objective well-being is typically aligned with phenomena that can be objectively measured, such as access to shelter, social care, food and education. It is external and can fluctuate with social, political and economic unrest.
>
> - Subjective well-being: On the other hand, subjective well-being can be less easy to measure as it is largely focused on experience, happiness and purpose. Subjective well-being can be considered an internal process, with some people able to frame challenging life events in a positive way, thus reducing their negative impact.
>
> When health and well-being come together, it can be considered that wellness is achieved.

found the number presenting with a clinically significant level of psychological distress increased from 20.8% in 2019 to 29.5% in April 2020, and then 24.5% in late March 2021.[4] On top of the social and health burden, the economic costs of mental illness in the UK have been estimated at £118 billion a year.[5] As a result, organisations are having to take a more active role in supporting both the physical and mental health of employees, further blurring the boundaries between personal mental well-being and professional work environments.

While a significant proportion of poor health and well-being outcomes is linked to culture and management practices, there is a rising appreciation of the role of the workplace in facilitating positive health outcomes and in providing nurturing environments from which to reach the upper levels of Maslow's hierarchical needs.[6]

HUMAN-CENTRIC DESIGN – A MORE NUANCED APPROACH

Just like personalities, no two bodies are the same. However, historically, offices and cities have been built assuming the physical dimensions of '50th percentile reference man': able-bodied, weighing 73kg and 173cm tall.[10] Everything from computer keyboards to office chairs and heating and cooling systems have been designed assuming a universal body dimension. With the rise of inclusive design has come a greater appreciation that these standardised dimensions not only represent a small percentage of the workforce, but that harm can be done by ignoring the need to accommodate the variety of body types at work.

Bodies are continuously shifting their sensitivity to stimulation. From temperature to acoustics, sight, light and more besides, each person will have a different response. Further, the human body does not stay static, experiencing both acute and chronic phases of good health conditions and poor, which can range from broken limbs and permanent physical change to pregnancy and menopause.

Inclusive, biomimetic design, with humans at its centre, must therefore cater for the broader range of bodies in the workplace, including differing:

- genders and gender identification
- age and life phases
- neurodiversity and disability

CASE STUDY 3.01

HMRC – Inclusive Design

LOCATION: UK

INTERIOR DESIGN: AECOM

HMRC's new hubs provide safe, modern and inclusive workspaces, enabling a culture where everyone feels valued.

Colin Cassé, HMRC's Director of Estates and Locations Programme, says,

Our regional centres, and phase one of the government hubs agenda, provide modern, inclusive working environments for our employees. These buildings ensure safe, welcoming and accessible environments to support better collaboration, productivity and well-being for all. Our inclusive design standards support all our employees to work in our buildings confidently, independently and with dignity.

Following the launch of its industry-leading 'Inclusive Design Guide' in 2019, HMRC was the first organisation to be awarded the Construction Industry Council's (CIC) Inclusive Environments Recognition certification. HMRC's Edinburgh Hub, Queen Elizabeth House, was the first building to receive accreditation.

In delivering its new workspaces, HMRC consulted workplace adjustment experts and staff networks – including the Neurodiversity Network – to gather input and feedback to make continual improvements. These customer perspectives enabled HMRC to influence how its architects, project managers, construction teams and furniture suppliers approached inclusivity. For example, in response to colleagues' concerns about the predominantly white colour and finishes in the workspaces, HMRC introduced a variety of colours and sensory-muted zones.

FURTHER INCLUSIVE DESIGN FEATURES INCLUDE:

- drop-off points and level access from accessible parking
- access to the building through power-operated, clam-shell doors
- different heights of reception desks, to accommodate people standing or sitting
- full knee recesses in reception desks and under kitchen units
- taps, sinks, appliances and cupboards at different heights
- controls for zip-taps positioned on the front face of the unit holding the tap
- 50% height-adjustable desking
- a range of desk colours and sensory-muted areas for neurodivergent workers
- universal showers and toilets
- side-mounted taps on the basins in the accessible toilets for ease of access
- a dog spend area for assistance dogs
- reflection rooms providing quiet spaces to pray or reflect

HMRC has delivered and occupied 17 new inclusive workplaces across the UK. The organisation has a dedicated team to develop, deliver, measure and champion its Inclusive Design Guide (IDG), building on, and where possible going further than, the existing British Standard, BS8300, 'Design of an accessible and inclusive built environment'; the Buildings Regulations, parts M and K ('Access to and use of buildings' and 'Protection from falling, collision and impact'); and the Equality Act 2010. HMRC monitors and measures the outcomes of its approach and uses lessons learnt to enhance future projects.

Focused on providing practical and easy-to-implement guidance on design materials, spatial compositions and workplace services, the IDG (see overleaf) seeks to provide safe, modern and inclusive workplaces enabling improved collaboration, smarter working and a culture where everyone feels valued.

HMRC IDG design approach

The IDG design approach is structured into four layers as shown in figure 3.03: facilities, entry and navigation, building approach, and culture and best practice.

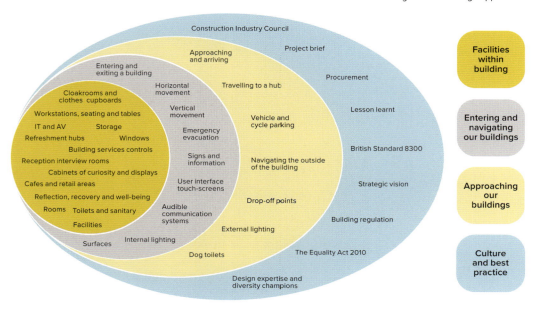

Figure 3.03: HMRC Inclusive Design Guide – design approach

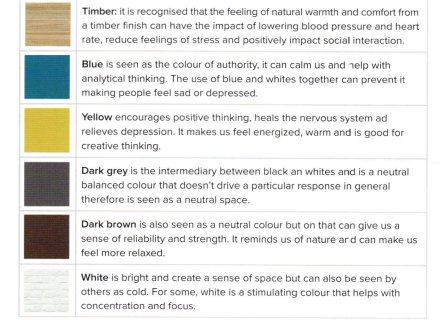

	Timber: it is recognised that the feeling of natural warmth and comfort from a timber finish can have the impact of lowering blood pressure and heart rate, reduce feelings of stress and positively impact social interaction.
	Blue is seen as the colour of authority, it can calm us and help with analytical thinking. The use of blue and whites together can prevent it making people feel sad or depressed.
	Yellow encourages positive thinking, heals the nervous system ad relieves depression. It makes us feel energized, warm and is good for creative thinking.
	Dark grey is the intermediary between black an whites and is a neutral balanced colour that doesn't drive a particular response in general therefore is seen as a neutral space.
	Dark brown is also seen as a neutral colour but on that can give us a sense of reliability and strength. It reminds us of nature and can make us feel more relaxed.
	White is bright and create a sense of space but can also be seen by others as cold. For some, white is a stimulating colour that helps with concentration and focus.

Figure 3.04: Contrasting desk finishes in situ

Table 3.02: HMRC Inclusive Design Guide – desk finishes. The use of solid colour or natural material surfaces can help to reduce the transfer of bright light.

CHAPTER 3: THE IMPACT OF BUILDINGS ON WELL-BEING

Figure 3.05: Location signage on arrival

Figure 3.06: Themed floor-level concepts for wayfinding and orientation

Figure 3.07: Use of icons in signage

Figure 3.08: Inclusion of outdoor space

43

↑ Figure 3.09: Quiet booth

↞ Figure 3.10: Maximisation of views and natural light

↙ Figure 3.11: Acoustic and visual shielding

↓ Figure 3.12: Sensory-muted room

GENDER AND GENDER IDENTIFICATION

While 'reference man' has long been assumed as the universal employee, he does not represent all men, let alone all women. For example, women may require office chairs more suited to supporting their pelvic position, and specific design interventions to accommodate the pregnant or menopausal body. Therefore a significant opportunity exists to challenge the way that workplaces are designed and how they represent the lives, experiences and bodies of women at work. Gender identification is causing us to rethink access, signage and amenities such as gender-neutral toilets.

In addition to workplace design, the redevelopment of cities also presents the opportunity to recontextualise the historic living and working patterns of women through rethinking the proximity of work, home and childcare, residential planning and transportation. This has been shown to positively support the economic development of women worldwide.[11]

AGE, LIFE PHASES AND THE NEED FOR ALTERNATIVE WORK ENVIRONMENTS

As the average working age increases, so too must the understanding of the environmental needs for supporting optimal health in a range of ages and life phases.

Brain maturation takes place around 25 years old, with the prefrontal cortex, responsible for executive function and decision-making, being the last part to mature.[13] Several studies have suggested an increased sensitivity within the young adult brain to hyper-stimulating events, which may create susceptibility to distraction.[14] There is a growing body of research that focuses on how to create mind-friendly work environments that allow all brains and bodies to flourish, including technology-free spaces, a range of hypo- and hyper-stimulated environments and spaces for active rest and restoration.

Life stages that correspond with an increased level of stress, such as bereavement, may also benefit from space designed for 'rest and digest', such as meditation booths, biophilic environments or immersive sound experiences. In addition, the impact of indoor environmental quality (IEQ) has been shown to play a significant role in both psychological and physiological stress processes.[15]

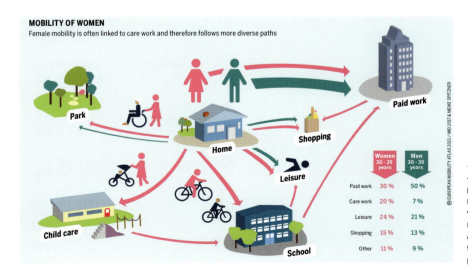

← Figure 3.13: Feminist Cities – Mobility of Women. Mobility patterns of women are largely more fragmented and higher in volume compared to men. As a result, women may be held at a financial disadvantage when travel fares do not represent point-to-point travel.[12]

NEURODIVERSITY AND THE WORKPLACE

Recent years have seen a proliferation of spaces designed for those who are neurodivergent. While additional attention is necessary for this previously under-considered employee group, a greater understanding of the definition of neurodiversity and corresponding environmental needs is required.

Neurodiversity refers to variations in human neurocognitive functioning – the different ways we think, process information and relate to ourselves and others. Mismatches between an individual's needs and their environments can create barriers and challenges to members of this community.

It is widely accepted that traits of neurodiversity are normally distributed across a population, with only those who reach a categorical threshold (and subsequent clinical diagnosis) defined as neurodivergent. Many work organisations focus on the disclosure of these categorical diagnoses to define who the space is for. However, there are several limiting factors in this approach:

- Focusing on the diagnosis and corresponding dedicated space may be stigmatising.
- The disclosure of a diagnosis is irrelevant to the need to provide spaces that cultivate productive work for all.
- Neurodiversity exists on a spectrum with differing symptoms, behavioural outcomes and input needs. Some people may require stimulating spaces to concentrate and others un-stimulating spaces.
- By providing spaces with a more diverse population in mind, employers will ultimately benefit the whole work community.
- Spaces designed to be mind-friendly help a range of mental and physical health states, personalities and working preferences.

In designing spaces, service-user inclusion is paramount, as neurodiverse and wider mental, physical and cognitive health issues are many and varied, with challenges ranging from stimulation factors through to accessibility and visual impairment.

CASE STUDY 3.02

HOK – Sensory Processing, Neurodiversity and Workplace Design

LOCATION: GLOBAL

There is growing recognition of the impact that workplace environments have on performance. This 'Sensory Processing, Neurodiversity and Workplace Design' report presents the latest research on what the key challenges are facing neuro-minorities and how businesses can help them thrive.

The study is a collaboration between HOK, a global architecture and design firm, and Tarkett North America, a global flooring manufacturer, with advice from Genius Within, an organisation dedicated to helping neuro-minorities maximise their potential.

The study explored what 202 neurodiverse individuals needed to help them thrive in the workplace – and what got in the way. The report also looks at any notable differences between gender, age and different types of diagnoses, and offers some practical tips on how to tackle these issues from a workplace-design perspective.

Findings from the research were:

- 47% of respondents identified as being hypersensitive, while 22% identified as hyposensitive.
- 57% noted a combination of neurodiverse conditions.
- The majority of respondents (77%) were hypersensitive to sound.
- Women reported more sensitivities across the board than men.
- Non-binary individuals were significantly more sensitive to their environment than men and women.
- Men felt less challenged by pattern, colour and textures than women.
- The 30- to 60-year-old age group needed more tactile input than other age groups.
- Delivering 'a choice of different space options' was the most popular strategy overall.

CHAPTER 3: THE IMPACT OF BUILDINGS ON WELL-BEING

Key learnings and/or design fundamentals

For any organisation to truly address inclusion, it needs to address operational issues, allow for personalised adjustments and address the built environment. There are a variety of strategies that can be leveraged to start to create space that is more inclusive and welcoming. The first is adopting the Universal Principles of Design, but there are also some additional, simple design interventions that can be deployed to make the space more equitable, functional and welcoming, including the following:

- Give people options to select where they will work.
- Design spaces that allow people to move.
- Enable access to natural elements, views and daylight.
- Provide access to quiet spaces and places to retreat to for refreshment and rejuvenation.
- Ensure there are energised areas people can engage with physically.
- Provide options and enable some degree of control over lighting, acoustics and temperature levels.
- Provide adjustable, ergonomic furniture.

Figures 3.14.a–f: HOK – Sensory processing and neurodiversity environmental elements

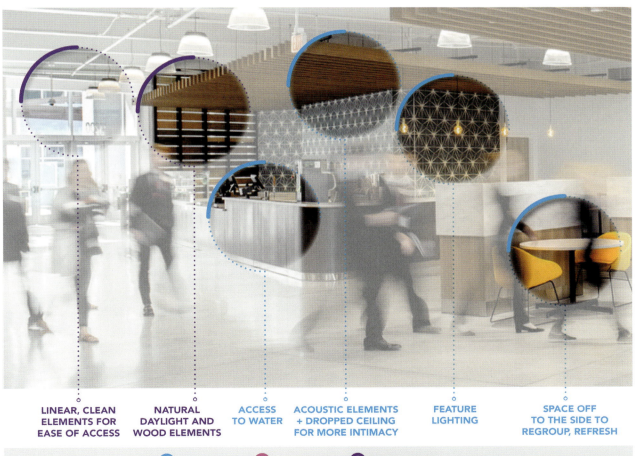

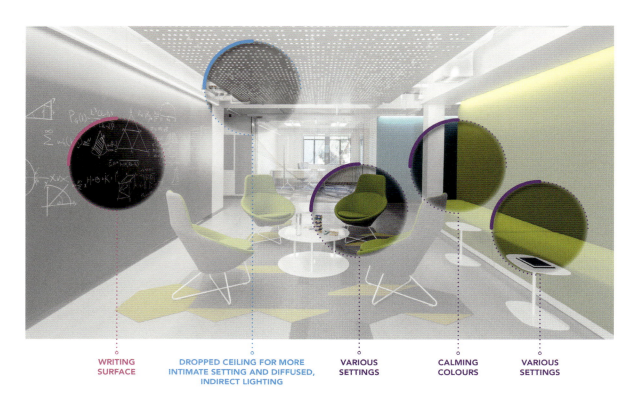

WRITING SURFACE | DROPPED CEILING FOR MORE INTIMATE SETTING AND DIFFUSED, INDIRECT LIGHTING | VARIOUS SETTINGS | CALMING COLOURS | VARIOUS SETTINGS

SMALL, INTIMATE SEATING | SOLO SEATING OPTIONS | OPTION FOR ACTIVE ENGAGEMENT | BOLD MATERIALITY, LIGHTING | SEATING NICHES

○ HYPER-SENSITIVE   ○ HYPO-SENSITIVE   ○ HYPER AND HYPO

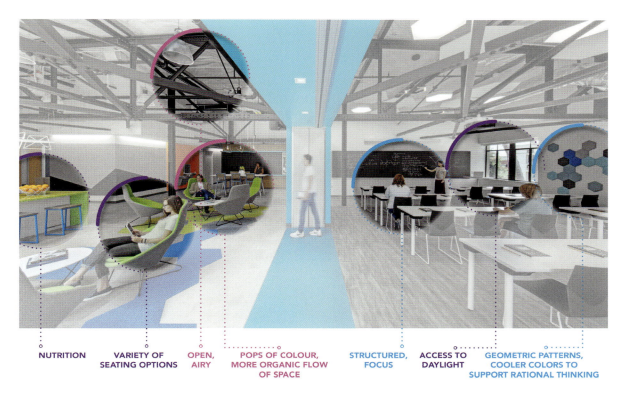

NUTRITION | VARIETY OF SEATING OPTIONS | OPEN, AIRY | POPS OF COLOUR, MORE ORGANIC FLOW OF SPACE | STRUCTURED, FOCUS | ACCESS TO DAYLIGHT | GEOMETRIC PATTERNS, COOLER COLORS TO SUPPORT RATIONAL THINKING

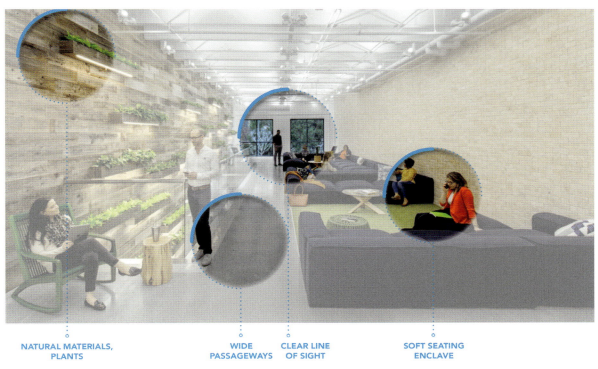

NATURAL MATERIALS, PLANTS | WIDE PASSAGEWAYS | CLEAR LINE OF SIGHT | SOFT SEATING ENCLAVE

○ HYPER-SENSITIVE ○ HYPO-SENSITIVE ○ HYPER AND HYPO

49

REWORKING THE WORKPLACE

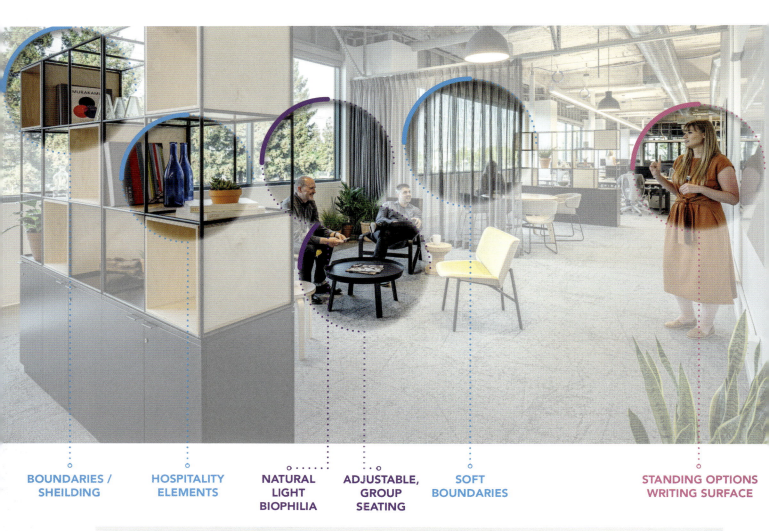

| BOUNDARIES / SHEILDING | HOSPITALITY ELEMENTS | NATURAL LIGHT BIOPHILIA | ADJUSTABLE, GROUP SEATING | SOFT BOUNDARIES | STANDING OPTIONS WRITING SURFACE |

○ HYPER-SENSITIVE   ○ HYPO-SENSITIVE   ○ HYPER AND HYPO

'If you've met one person with autism, you've met one person with autism.'

DR STEPHEN SHORE

CHAPTER 3: THE IMPACT OF BUILDINGS ON WELL-BEING

CASE STUDY 3.03

Maggie's Centres

LOCATIONS: VARIOUS, UK AND INTERNATIONAL

In response to growing concerns about well-being in the office, inspiration is being sought in some healthcare settings where design is delivering more supportive environments.

The network of Maggie's Centres — now with 24 across the UK and three internationally, most recently in Hong Kong — are exemplary in their focus on uplifting visitors: people living with cancer, and their family and friends. They are often small in scale, designed with a variety of collaborative and contemplative spaces featuring natural materials, sunlight and ventilation. Each centre is integrated with nature, always with access to outside spaces, thoughtfully planted to reflect the changing seasons. The design remit embraces ways of ensuring that the needs and well-being of staff are cared for too.

The drop-in centres are funded and run by a charity founded by the late Maggie Keswick Jencks, who died of cancer and who wanted to create welcoming, friendly and caring places where people with cancer could feel comfortable about accessing support, information and practical advice.

Located in the grounds of major NHS hospitals, the centres have been designed by high-profile architects and designers including Frank Gehry, Foster + Partners, Snøhetta and Heatherwick Studio. Their outstanding, individual designs stand in contrast with the hospitals in many ways, but primarily by ensuring that the centres focus on the patient and staff instead of the disease. The centres acted as welcome oases of calm and recovery for NHS staff during the pandemic.

The buildings of Maggie's centres are designed to support and inspire our visitors and staff. Each centre gives a feeling of "I can imagine feeling different here". The buildings work in harmony with our staff's professional skills which enables positive culture and behaviours. The designs mean the internal and external world are aligned which activates the senses and gives energy and curiosity to every person who visits.

DAME LAURA LEE, OBE

Figure 3.15: Maggie's Centre, Leeds, by Heatherwick Studio — harmonious architecture and landscaping

KEY FEATURES OF THE CENTRES

- connection to nature, access to outside spaces, ideally a garden or courtyard
- a welcoming and friendly entrance with no formal reception desk and views into the building – a space for first-time visitors to pause and take in initial impressions of the place
- the kitchen as the hub for each centre – with a large table and opportunities for people to help themselves to refreshments and meet others. A friendly place for exchange, whether that's stories of cancer or nutrition classes
- a library and computers for visitors, their friends and families to research, discover and be quiet
- discrete staff offices and consulting rooms to ensure the majority of the centre's space remains non-institutional
- sitting rooms of different sizes for workshops, classes or talking by the fire
- high ceilings and rooflights, where appropriate, to provide a generous sense of space. Focus on quality and a positive visitor experience; traditional calculations of costs per square metre tend not to embrace the value and positive aspects of volume and quality of space
- generous use of natural, durable materials – many materials are selected to age well, and the high specification has reaped rewards by reducing the need for regular refurbishment
- plenty of natural light, ventilation and views out, to ensure that staff and visitors can follow the natural circadian rhythms of the day and do not spend time in artificially lit environments

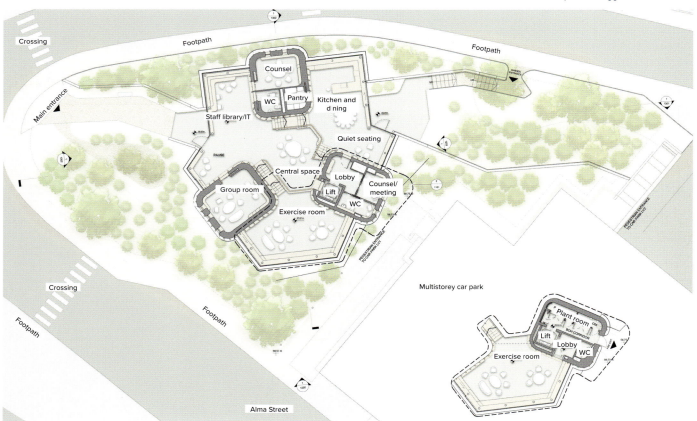

Figure 3.16: Ground-floor plan of Maggie's Centre, Leeds

Figure 3.17: A welcoming entry experience at Maggie's Centre, Charing Cross Hospital, London, by Ab Rogers Design

Figure 3.18: Providing space for people to connect with nature at Maggie's Centre, Manchester, by Foster + Partners

CONCLUSION

The experience of being human is individual and personal. While most organisations are not structured to manage individual preferences, a greater appreciation and spatial representation of human differences can not only provide a more conducive environment for individuals to thrive, but also dramatically improve health and well-being. Regardless of the increase in hybrid and remote working, the office is key to delivering many of the physical, social, intellectual and environmental interventions that support human health and the ensuing productivity and engagement. As people spend a third of their lives at work, setting the right foundations for health within the office is critical.[16]

Looking to the future, there is a significant opportunity for private practice and academic institutions to collaborate on further developing the understanding of how environments inform neurological, cognitive and behavioural processes, in both face-to-face and digital interactions. Once there is a greater understanding of environmental neuropsychology and its ability to facilitate great work, truly human-centric design solutions can be explored.

LEARNING POINTS

- To successfully design buildings to facilitate and nurture humans and their diverse needs, a greater understanding is required of what these needs are.
- While health and well-being are often synonymous, there are clear distinctions, which have a differing impact on the design process.
- Health is 'a state of complete physical, mental and social well-being and not merely the absence of disease or infirmity'.
- Just like personalities, no two bodies are the same; there is a greater appreciation that the standard dimensions of 'reference man' do not represent the workforce and there is a growing need to accommodate different bodies at work.
- A significant opportunity exists to challenge the way in which offices are designed and whether they represent the lives, experiences and bodies of women at work.
- Different ages and life-phases need different environments. Our bodies and brains are not static. An environment conducive to good cognitive and physical health is different in childhood compared to at retirement.
- Some life stages, such as having a young family or experiencing bereavement, correspond with an increased level of stress. People may benefit from space designed to engage the para-sympathetic nervous system to counteract their 'fight or flight', stress-induced state.
- For office environments to support the basis of what it means to be human and to achieve states of health and well-being, designers and architects need to understand and cater to these needs.
- Well-being is an ongoing process and multi-dimensional; it is not a single event or service.
- To create optimal environments for health and well-being to flourish, designers should address the Eight Dimensions of Wellness.
- Well-being at work directly impacts engagement and productivity.

CHAPTER 4

Delivering positive social impact

INTRODUCTION

There is no shortage of examples throughout history of organisations 'doing the right thing', placing the planet and social good before profit. Whether it is through the provision of social housing for the 'labouring poor' (Peabody, Bourneville, Cadbury), or more recent examples of planet-friendly consumer goods (Patagonia, Unilever), the drive for organisations to give back to the planet and its populations is accelerating.

The latest evolution of this concern is rooted in recent fuel, food and climate crises that have highlighted the need for increasing environmental and social awareness in how we live our lives. The response has been the rise of interest in an organisation's environmental, social and governance (ESG) performance. ESG is very much at the heart of the financial and political markets and the construction industry (with the built environment responsible for around 40% of emissions), as well as becoming a mission for Gen Z.[1]

While all three ESG elements are inextricably linked, to date most focus has been on the environmental impacts of business and how they can be reduced. However, in the post-pandemic era, social sustainability, the ability to endure and thrive, is now rapidly climbing the agenda. This chapter explores how the real estate sector can play a key role in supporting and delivering positive social impact through the workplace.

WHAT IS SOCIAL IMPACT AND SOCIAL SUSTAINABILITY?

The foundations for today's global approach to sustainability were laid in the late 1980s with the publication of a report titled *Our Common Future*.[2] A critical message of the document was the idea that global environmental problems stemmed from unsustainable consumption and production in the northern hemisphere and poverty in the southern. From the report also came a people-focused definition of sustainable development as 'development that meets the needs of the present without compromising the ability of future generations to meet their own needs'.

The document has subsequently become more widely known as the Brundtland Report. Written by Gro Harlem Brundtland, the chairwoman of the World Commission on Environment and Development, it developed guiding principles for sustainable development that continue to be relevant today.

A quarter of a century on, the United Nations (UN) defines social sustainability as being about 'identifying and managing business impacts, both positive and negative, on people'. It continues, 'As part of this, the quality of a company's relationships and engagement with its stakeholders is critical. Directly or indirectly, companies affect what happens to employees, workers in the value chain, customers and local communities, and it is important to manage impacts proactively.'[3]

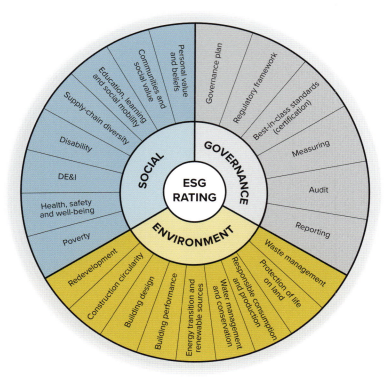

↞ Figure 4.01: The built environment and the ESG wheel

CHAPTER 4: DELIVERING POSITIVE SOCIAL IMPACT

As a key player in people's lives and the future of the planet, business globally is increasingly being asked to adopt more responsible operations and strategies to align with areas including human rights, the environment and labour laws. The Covid-19 pandemic underlined the importance of organisations in playing an active role not just in the well-being of their workers but more broadly in their communities as a positive presence and good neighbour.

THE UN'S PRINCIPLES AND SUSTAINABLE DEVELOPMENT GOALS

As part of its role as a global convener, the UN's Global Compact provides corporate sustainability guidance for businesses to adopt socially responsible and sustainable policies. The Ten Principles for business embrace human rights, labour, the environment and anti-corruption. In addition, the UN's Global Compact is driving business awareness and action to help achieve the 17 Sustainable Development Goals (SDGs).

THE TEN PRINCIPLES

The Ten Principles of the United Nations Global Compact are derived from: the Universal Declaration of Human Rights, the International Labour Organization's Declaration on Fundamental Principles and Rights at Work, the Rio Declaration on Environment and Development, and the United Nations Convention Against Corruption.[4]

HUMAN RIGHTS

Principle 1: Businesses should support and respect the protection of internationally proclaimed human rights; and

Principle 2: make sure that they are not complicit in human rights abuses.

LABOUR

Principle 3: Businesses should uphold the freedom of association and the effective recognition of the right to collective bargaining;

Principle 4: the elimination of all forms of forced and compulsory labour;

Principle 5: the effective abolition of child labour; and

Principle 6: the elimination of discrimination in respect of employment and occupation.

Figure 4.02: Sustainable Development Goals, United Nations

ENVIRONMENT

Principle 7: Businesses should support a precautionary approach to environmental challenges;

Principle 8: undertake initiatives to promote greater environmental responsibility; and

Principle 9: encourage the development and diffusion of environmentally friendly technologies.

ANTI-CORRUPTION

Principle 10: Businesses should work against corruption in all its forms, including extortion and bribery.

HOW TO DELIVER POSITIVE SOCIAL IMPACT THROUGH REAL ESTATE

By combining the UN ambitions, it's possible to identify social sustainability goals that relate directly to the real estate sector and the built environment. These can be summarised as follows:

1. **Ensuring healthy lives and human rights:** promoting well-being through a combination of SDG 3 ('Ensure healthy lives and promote well-being for all at all ages') and Principle 1, concerning human rights.

2. **Promoting sustainable economic growth:** encouraging job creation and prosperity through SDG 8 ('Promote sustained, inclusive and sustainable economic growth, full and productive employment and decent work for all'), in combination with Principle 3, on workers' rights

3. **Fostering resilience and innovation:** improving quality of life through SDG 9 ('Build resilient infrastructure, promote inclusive and sustainable industrialisation and foster innovation') and Principle 9, on encouraging environmentally friendly technologies

4. **Supporting inclusivity and equity:** promoting social fairness and decency through SDG 11 ('Make cities and human settlements inclusive, safe, resilient and sustainable') and Principle 4, on eliminating forced and compulsory labour

5. **Building social resilience:** enabling social sustainability through addressing climate change via SDG 13 ('Take urgent action to combat climate change and its impacts'), in combination with Principle 8, on promoting initiatives for greater environmental responsibility

6. **Creating inclusive societies and sustainable development:** creating socially sustainable communities through SDG 16 ('Promote peaceful and inclusive societies for sustainable development') and Principle 6, for the elimination of discrimination in respect of employment and occupation.

ENSURING HEALTHY LIVES AND HUMAN RIGHTS

When it comes to social sustainability and governance there remain challenges in measuring the positive impact of various actions. With the spotlight on these two areas there are starting to emerge an array of measurement tools; see case study 4.01. The Urban Mind Project was conceived to help promote well-being through understanding how people respond to their environments. The app has provided empirical support for the notion that nature can have measurable beneficial effects on mental well-being.

CHAPTER 4: DELIVERING POSITIVE SOCIAL IMPACT

CASE STUDY 4.01

Urban Mind Project

LOCATION: KING'S CROSS, LONDON, UK

RESEARCH TEAM: KING'S COLLEGE LONDON, J&L GIBBONS AND NOMAD PROJECTS

As increasing numbers of people live in urban areas, the negative implications are growing for global mental health. However, while it is recognised that city dwellers are at a higher risk of mental illness, an increasing body of evidence suggests that natural features within the built environment can counteract the effects of urban living and even promote good mental health.

To explore the effects of nature in the city, the Urban Mind Project, co-developed by King's College London, landscape architects J&L Gibbons and arts foundation Nomad Projects, wanted to address the question 'what elements of being in nature affect mood and subsequent mental-health issues?'

The research consortium developed a smartphone-based tool that questioned participants on their immediate environmental surroundings. By asking questions such as 'can you see or hear birds?' together with 'to what degree do you feel happy/stressed/worried?', the researchers were able to collect a significant body of data.

To increase the participation and 'gamification' of the research, participants are asked to take a photo of their feet and the underlying ground. These photos of the ground beneath the feet of the participants were intended to create a sense of the mosaic of the urban fabric.

Results from the initial research included:

- Significant associations with positive mental well-being were associated with factors such as being outdoors, seeing trees and feeling in touch with nature.
- Beneficial effects could still be observed even if the participant was no longer outdoors and no longer had access to nature. This lagged effect indicated a time-lasting impact of nature on mental well-being.

Implications of this research:

The findings provided empirical support for the notion that short-term exposure to specific natural features can have measurable beneficial effects on mental well-being. The investigation suggested that the benefits of nature on mental well-being were time-lasting and interacted with an individual's vulnerability to mental illness.

Figure 4.03: A participant photographs their immediate surroundings.

Figure 4.04: The mosaic of urban fabric

59

PROMOTING SUSTAINABLE ECONOMIC GROWTH

As part of a systematic shift in the way in which modern businesses are designed and managed, more organisations are signing up to the strict business protocols required by B Corp. By October 2022, 5,866 companies globally had signed up to voluntarily achieve the highest environmental and social standards to lead global change; to design inclusive, equitable and regenerative economies; and to build a resilient future for all of humanity. The likely impact of this on the built environment and workplaces is significant. This will manifest both in terms of requirements for buildings to reach the highest standards, but also through the brand communication of organisational values, providing an opportunity to attract and retain the best talent. See case study 4.02 for how the FORE Partnership incorporates social values in its approach to real estate.

CASE STUDY 4.02

FORE Partnership

LOCATION: VARIOUS, UK

For FORE Partnership, ESG is in its DNA. Established to achieve higher investment returns in real estate by supercharging positive social and environmental change, FORE became one of the first property firms to certify as a B Corporation.

In becoming a B Corp, FORE legally committed to pursue purpose beyond profit. It is part of a global community of firms committed to harnessing the power of business to help address society's greatest challenges and to build a more inclusive economy. In real estate terms this is an exemplar of connecting people, purpose and place.

The 10-storey Cadworks building is the first net-zero office in Glasgow and one of the most sustainable buildings in Scotland. Through projects like this, FORE is delivering on its mission to be an industry leader in tackling the climate crisis and a catalyst for positive outcomes when working with grassroots organisations or larger social enterprises that make an enormous difference to communities.

➤ Figure 4.05: Cadworks in Glasgow – the reception area

CHAPTER 4: DELIVERING POSITIVE SOCIAL IMPACT

FOSTERING RESILIENCE AND INNOVATION

Improving quality of life relies on resilience and innovation, and by bringing together start-ups and academia the Enterprise Centre in Norwich provides high-quality workspace, networking and knowledge-sharing in an inspiring setting; see case study 4.03.

CASE STUDY 4.03

Enterprise Centre, University of East Anglia

LOCATION: NORWICH, UK

ARCHITECT: ARCHITYPE

COMPLETION: 2015

UEA Enterprise Centre is the first building to achieve Passive House design standard in education. It was one of 17 buildings globally highlighted as best practice at COP26.

Figure 4.06: Enterprise Centre, University of East Anglia – thatched external wall

Bio-based materials used throughout ensure the building is almost entirely reusable or recyclable. From the thatched roof – pre-built by a master thatcher and feathered together on site – to the recycled newspaper ceiling and external timber cladding made from recycled chemistry lab benches, the building's character is communicated through each surface.

The three-year post-occupancy evaluation indicates that the building will not only create a 70% reduction in carbon compared to other university buildings, but it will perform as new for the next 100 years.

◂◂ Figure 4.07: Cafe and workspace. Use of local suppliers, craftspeople and materials resulted in low material replacement cycles.

▸▸ Figure 4.08: Co-working space. Biomass district heating (pellets or wood) in combination with intentionally designed natural ventilation ensures that the building is able to passively maintain a comfortable temperature 365 days a year. The building provides a local incubator community for start-ups spinning out of academia.

CHAPTER 4: DELIVERING POSITIVE SOCIAL IMPACT

SUPPORTING INCLUSIVITY AND EQUITY

Promoting social fairness and decency, the social enterprise hub Sydney NGO Precinct is home to a collection of organisations with the focus of fighting poverty.

CASE STUDY 4.04

Sydney NGO Precinct and Social Enterprise Hub

LOCATION: SYDNEY, AUSTRALIA

COMPLETION: 2025

Demonstrating the value of public space as critical social infrastructure, an innovative, campus-style, social-enterprise hub is helping to breathe new life into an urban park in Sydney. The hub is a place where non-profit organisations, social enterprises and micro-enterprises work together to reduce poverty and build community.

Called the Sydney NGO Precinct and Social Enterprise Hub, the project is focused on reusing and restoring nineteenth-century heritage-listed sanatorium buildings and open spaces. The pathways, courtyards, colonnades and lawns provide an exceptional urban setting for the hub and its 40 non-governmental organisations (NGOs) related to health and well-being combined with employment and learning opportunities.

Workers at the scheme will share services and common facilities, working together to deliver outcomes aligned with the UN sustainable development goals. The project and its grounds will welcome the public as part of the major urban parkland.

The project will adapt and activate empty heritage buildings and grounds for a wide range of organisations and events with a common purpose. It will demonstrate how historic buildings with embedded energy can be adapted to be permanently and sustainably useful with minimal environmental impact.

The idea creates the first social enterprise venture of its kind in Australia, an innovation that has proven success and social benefits in other countries. It has been estimated that over A$500 million (£285 million) in economic, health and social benefits could be returned to the community over the 10-year programme. The project will deliver benefits quickly at low cost because the buildings are already adaptable. This will minimise delays and expensive alteration, compliance and upgrade works that would be required in a major change of use.

This project highlights the value of public space as social infrastructure similar to schools, hospitals, public transport, roads and so on. It is a compatible, low-impact and low-cost use for the existing facilities, already made habitable with major capital investment over time, and is an affordable and easy placemaking opportunity with immediate community benefits.

◂◂ Figure 4.09: Old sanatorium building repurposed for a social cause within an urban park in Sydney

63

BUILDING SOCIAL RESILIENCE

Taking the full set of the UN's SDGs as its inspiration, the SDG House in Amsterdam accommodates organisations and individuals working to deliver social sustainability through addressing climate change; see case study 4.05.

CASE STUDY 4.05

SDG House

LOCATION: AMSTERDAM, THE NETHERLANDS

In its landmark building in Amsterdam, SDG House provides space for more than 70 professionals and entrepreneurs to connect and work together to achieve the UN's SDGs. Highlighting the value of public space as social infrastructure, the SDG House was the idea of the Dutch Royal Tropical Institute known as Koninklijk Institut voor de Tropen (KIT).

When KIT had its national subsidy reduced, it started renting out the property to impact-driven organisations, profit and non-profit. The rental price is in line with the market and is a source of income for KIT, just like the hotel, restaurant and event spaces. These sources of income ensure that KIT is self-sustaining.

SDG House member De Gezonde Stad is committed to creating a healthy and sustainable Amsterdam. It has several sustainability projects and initiatives all around the city and helps companies and residents with their sustainability projects. From greening streets and squares, and reducing and reusing waste, to promoting locally produced food, it works extensively with the local community and existing initiatives. Since becoming an SDG House member, De Gezonde Stad has often worked with KIT, including to create a community garden on the campus.

Since its launch in 2017, KIT has delivered benefits quickly at low cost because the buildings were already well suited to adaptation for the intended purpose. It is a compatible, low-impact and low-cost use for a heritage building, already made habitable with major capital investment and embedded energy and resources over time.

Figure 4.10: SDG House – the outdoor green space

Figure 4.11: The SDG House entrance area

CREATING INCLUSIVE SOCIETIES AND SUSTAINABLE DEVELOPMENT

The roles of urban planners, architects and workplace professionals will become increasingly focused on how to address the inherent social inequality that exists at work. Work itself has a huge bearing on society and its inhabitants including wealth distribution, social mobility, wellness and mental health. How organisations facilitate relationships within their workforce, the societies that they work in, and the wider social environment is at the heart of creating socially sustainable communities. See case study 4.06 for how the HALO Enterprise and Innovation Centre addresses the quartet of social sustainability issues in an innovative new community.

CASE STUDY 4.06

HALO Net zero and Co-working

LOCATION: KILMARNOCK, SCOTLAND, UK

ARCHITECT: KEPPIE DESIGN

COMPLETION: 2022

With a vision for a dynamic commercial, educational, cultural and leisure quarter where people can 'live, work, learn and play', the HALO Enterprise and Innovation Centre (HEIC) in Kilmarnock provides a sustainable community approach to a mixed-use development, creating 1,500 jobs as well as training opportunities, economic growth, clean energy and 210 smart homes.

It is the first net-zero mixed-use development in Scotland. From autonomous electric vehicles to over 100 rooftop solar panels, the centre is to be fuelled by renewable energy. With almost £1.5 million invested in high-tech, smart energy equipment, there is a solar carport, 12 electric vehicle chargers, 10 zero-emission e-bikes and chargers, an electric bus, and a world-class battery storage unit. The use of sustainable modes of transport will be encouraged and reinforced by proximity to Kilmarnock train station and town centre.

Some 14 years in the making, driven by founder and executive chair Dr Marie Macklin, the HALO Kilmarnock is a £65 million brownfield urban-regeneration project on a 9.3-hectare (23-acre) site (formerly the home of Johnnie Walker whisky) designed to maximise collaboration between entrepreneurs and UK PLCs.

The first phase of development, the HALO Enterprise and Innovation Centre (HEIC), is home to a Barclays Eagle Lab supporting start-up and scale-up businesses from across Ayrshire that are building and growing specialised digital and cyber businesses. Platinum partner ScottishPower will use the HEIC for staff training, to host events and to support growing businesses on the HALO trading floor, establishing the HALO at the forefront of the digital 'Fourth Industrial Revolution'.

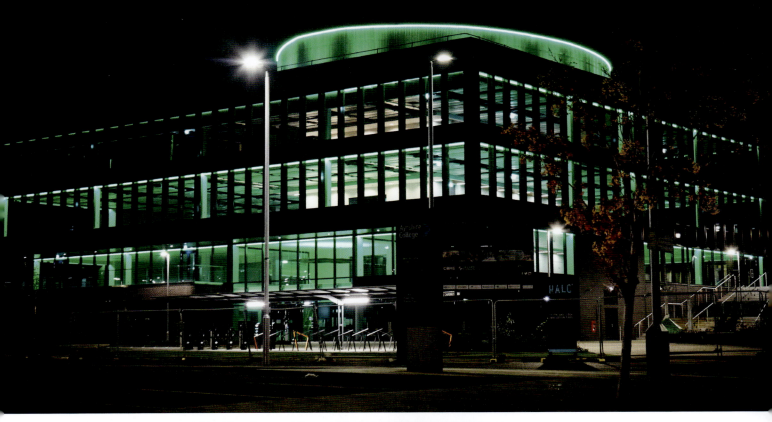

▲ Figure 4.12: HALO Enterprise Innovation Hub

◂◂ Figure 4.13: Aerial plan of HALO including green homes and workplaces for entrepreneurs. Phase two is under way, delivering 210 next-generation green homes for entrepreneurs while they grow their businesses and use HALO's live-work studios, Rock-Cribs. Fuelled by 100% renewable energy and with digital healthcare-monitoring systems, the homes will be constructed with sustainable materials and techniques, and used by ScottishPower as a testbed for smart, sustainably powered homes.

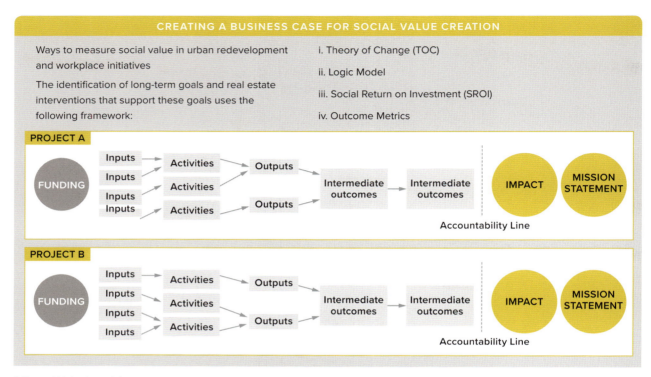

↑ Figure 4.14: Logic model example framework

CASE STUDY 4.07

Sea Containers House

LOCATION: SOUTH BANK, LONDON, UK

ARCHITECT: BDG

Communication and advertising company WPP repurposed a hotel to create light, innovative office space for their creative teams to thrive.

↠ Figure 4.15: Large open volumes with connecting accommodation stairs allow unobstructed daylight into workspaces.

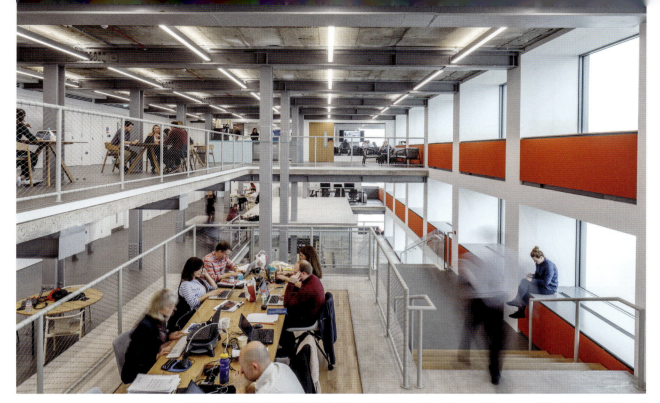

⌃ Figure 4.16: Open atrium with project space. Lighting from a high-level ceiling reaches deeper parts of the floor plate.

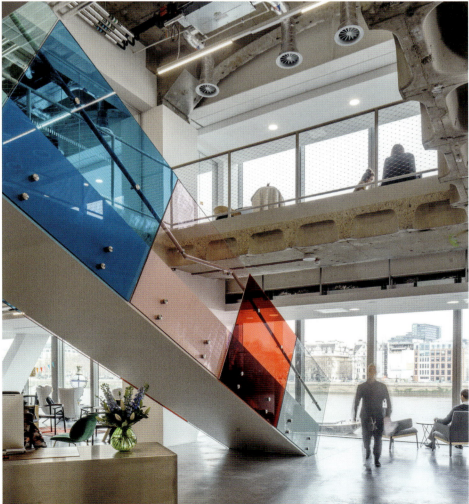

↠ Figure 4.17: Substantial slab cut-outs enable visual connection and light penetration throughout.

↑ Figure 4.19: Outdoor terraces connect the indoor environment with spectacular views of London.

← Figure 4.18: Vertical connections between floors for light and movement

CONCLUSION

ESG is the issue of our time. The built environment must reduce embodied carbon by reusing and repurposing office buildings, focusing on circularity, renewables, supporting local supply chains and resources. Buildings are the setting for community; they support inclusion, well-being, social and economic regeneration. However, neither the 'S' nor the 'E' can be effective without clear and measurable governance.

LEARNING POINTS

- The implications of social sustainability on *people* include:
  a. Addressing poverty through local hubs that reduce commuting, whilst offices remain accessible in order to reduce personal fuel bills at home
  b. Ensuring health, safety and well-being are central to every workplace experience
  c. The evaluation of how to design inclusive environments that reflect the totality of our current and future workforce, including those with disabilities
  d. Leveraging organisations, purchasing power through developing diverse supply chains and working more with minority-owned businesses
  e. Leveraging space to promote public and private connections and education and learning as a route to social mobility
  f. Creating business cases for social value creation to connect aspirations with tactical actions

- The implications of social sustainability on *purpose* include:
  a. ESG as a critical value driver for people and as a route to talent attraction and retention
  b. The acceleration of the number of companies pursuing a change, e.g. through B Corp certification

- The implications of social sustainability on *place* include:
  a. The need for urban planning to recontextualise historic inequalities without gentrifying environments and worsening inequality
  b. Leveraging space to create social innovation and collaboration hubs

PART II

PURPOSE

Workers are seeking jobs which provide a social purpose rather than just a paycheque. Similarly, consumers are buying products which speak to their ethical values rather than just performing functional requirements. If it is the purpose of place to respond to these factors, then how we design and manage our buildings must inevitably change.

CHAPTER 5

Operationalising the workplace experience

INTRODUCTION

With many workers expressing a clear preference for working at home most of the time, the office needs to work harder than ever to entice them back. The promise of a daily fruit bowl and a weekly yoga class no longer cuts it.

While a small proportion of companies have decided to divest themselves entirely of physical offices, the majority are exploring how best to enhance the experience of their real estate. The reasons to invest are numerous – to provide a physical focus for the workforce, to embody brand, to provide collaboration and social spaces and more. Underpinning all of this is the critical business case for attracting and retaining talent, which accounts for the greatest proportion of expenditure for all organisations.

Inspiration for how to rethink the workplace, particularly the office, is being drawn from many quarters, with the richest seam of ideas found in the retail and hospitality sectors – where the bar is set high when it comes to providing enjoyable and memorable experiences.

WHAT IS WORKPLACE EXPERIENCE AND WHY DO WE NEED IT?

While there is no agreed definition of 'workplace experience', there are some widely recognised traits. At its simplest, the workplace is a unit of space allocated for the purpose of getting work done, and experience is a human condition. A workplace with no people offers little in the way of experience. Therefore, we are defining workplace experience as the 'aggregated touchpoints connecting people, purpose and place'. And when these touchpoints combine to provide an enjoyable, stimulating and productive experience they make a visit to the office worthwhile, and sometimes even essential.

According to Jim Gilmore and Joe Pine, authors of *The Experience Economy*, 'time is the currency of experience' and people value experience based on the perceived time-benefit offered:[1]

- **Time well saved** is where the experience is centred on saving time not just resources.
- **Time well spent** focuses on whether the experience captures people's attention and they then value the time spent.
- **Time well invested** helps people achieve a broader aspiration.

Based on the 'currency of experience' description above, people may choose to work from home if they can do so efficiently and their priority is 'time well saved'. However, they will choose to travel to the office if it offers an experience that cannot be met elsewhere and is considered time well spent or invested, resulting in a

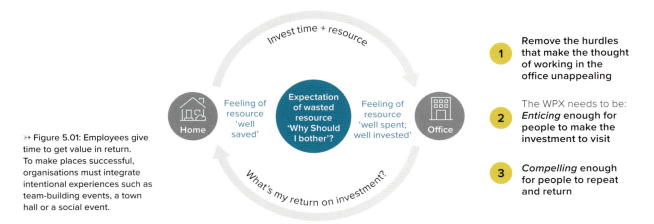

» Figure 5.01: Employees give time to get value in return. To make places successful, organisations must integrate intentional experiences such as team-building events, a town hall or a social event.

perceived positive return on the investment of the time and money it costs to go there.

In simple terms, employees give time to get value in return. If they are going to invest two hours in a commute, they must get more value from the workplace experience in the office than they do from working at home.

FROM MECHANICS TO HUMANICS

The traditional workplace experience has been about getting the mechanics right – for example, providing good-quality workstations or efficient IT support. However, now that people can choose where, when and how they work there also needs to be a focus on the 'humanics' of the experience, so that people will feel time is well spent when they work in the office.

Figure 5.02 shows the attributes contributing to how people feel about an experience. The foundation of all positive experiences is functionality; they must perform as intended. Contextual experiences make life easier and can often be automated or digitised. These first two layers are about the 'mechanics' of an experience. Moving up the pyramid, meaningful experiences are increasingly positive as they exceed expectations and leave us craving more; these layers are human-centric and focus on the 'humanics' of the experience.

CASE STUDY: 5.01
WeWork XSF

LOCATION: GLOBAL

As organisations and companies are seeking to respond to the changing wants and needs of workers, insights have been collected in a new global survey. Cushman & Wakefield partnered with WeWork to develop a workplace experience report, surveying 800 people working in WeWork spaces in London, Singapore and New York.

The research has shown that new, post-pandemic work patterns are evolving. Employees say they are likely to increase their time in flexible office spaces and reduce remote time spent at home or in third places such as libraries or coffee shops. This demonstrates that flexible offices are clearly a prominent and viable option in such an ecosystem. They have many of the same benefits as the traditional company office, and in some categories can offer additional benefits that match the new hybrid approach.

The top three reasons why employees recommend flexible office space are:

1. The space feels like an extension of the employee's traditional office and culture.
2. The space supports the employee's well-being.
3. The location offers the right technology and right spaces for collaboration.[2]

Figure 5.02: Workplace experience model (WPX)

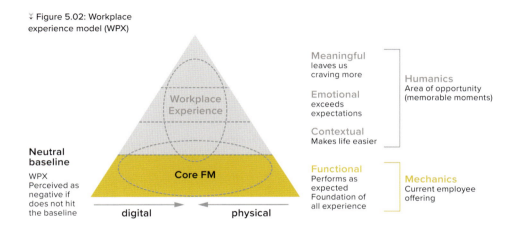

> **WHAT IS THE FUTURE OF FM?**
>
> The facilities management (FM) role was traditionally focused on catering to the 'mechanics' of the workplace experience. The role was largely invisible, only being noticed when something went wrong, but it has now evolved to include the delivery of hosting, cleaning and hospitality services. The value of FM was highlighted during the Covid-19 pandemic when the office experience focused on the health and safety of employees. Out-of-hours services, such as cleaning, suddenly became visible – for example, printed messages from the FM team were left on desks to confirm that the surfaces had been sterilised in order to make people feel safe.
>
> Looking to the future, FM teams, or 'workplace-experience teams' as they are often now described, are ideally placed to assist management in 'operationalising the workplace'. This means optimising the experience opportunities, both mechanic and humanic.
>
> With access to the correct data, FM and workplace teams will be able to identify potential savings and areas of opportunity in response to new patterns of workplace behaviour and occupation. They will be able make informed recommendations about how savings can be reallocated or redeployed to better align the workplace experience to employee needs, business culture and environmental, social and governance performance. This may result in the curation of new experiences for greeting and meeting or dynamic occupation strategies to respond to utilisation peaks and troughs. The emerging focus on staging and curating positive and memorable workplace experiences will increase the need to recruit the right personalities, particularly in employee-facing roles, and to introduce new measures of success that are less about operational excellence and more about delivering customer delight.

THE POWER OF HUMANICS

An example of rethinking customer service can be found with Zappos, the US online shoe retailer. Its mission is to provide 'the very best customer service, customer experience, and company culture. We aim to inspire the world by showing it's possible to simultaneously deliver **happiness** to customers, employees, vendors, shareholders, and the community in a long-term, sustainable way.'[3]

The Zappos customer service agents don't follow scripts; they are not measured on tickets resolved and response times; instead they are measured by net promoter scores – a mechanism used to gauge customer loyalty, satisfaction and personal service levels. For more on Zappos, read *Delivering Happiness: A Path to Profits, Passion and Purpose,* by founder Tony Hsieh.[4]

Tim Greenhalgh, Chief Creative Officer at brand and design specialist Landor & Fitch, believes that good experiences include a balance of physical, human and digital elements. It is important to align these attributes with the type of workplace experience being designed and curated, to ensure the desired output is achieved. A simple frictionless action designed to save time can be purely digital and will only be remembered for its efficiency: for example, an app to locate a colleague, swipe access and so on. However, other meaningful experiences should include a human element.

POSITIVE HUMAN EXPERIENCE VIA A DIGITAL MEDIUM

Blended human and digital experiences can be highly effective when designed well. For example, imagine giving an important hybrid presentation, with colleagues joining in the room and online but with people struggling to connect to the technology and start the meeting. In an old-style scenario, there were laminated sheets giving generic instructions on how to connect, and a helpdesk number. In an improved scenario, set-up assistance is requested when the room is booked. Logging into the meeting room automatically sets up a connection with a remote helpdesk assistant. They give a warm greeting, walk through the set-up and assist with any requirements. Meeting details are confirmed along with catering requirements and, should they be needed, additional cables and devices can be retrieved from the automated vending system outside the meeting room. This is an example of human experience in a physical space delivered through an efficient digital medium. An example of digital integration is the pop-up, self-service kiosk concept developed by Landor & Fitch for Singtel, one of Asia's leading telecommunications companies; see case study 5.02. 'Unboxed' reimagines the future of physical service points, including mobile stores, a future which seamlessly blends state-of-the-art physical, human and digital elements across different formats.

CASE STUDY 5.02
Unboxed by Singtel

LOCATION: COMCENTRE, SINGAPORE

DESIGN: LANDOR & FITCH

The design team focused on the idea of 'shaping your connected world'. The space features:

- the latest in security and health sensors at intuitive, interactive touchpoints
- facial recognition to ensure precisely personalised experiential design throughout
- intelligent wi-fi, enabling staff to locate and serve customers wherever they are in the manned stores, while in unmanned formats service staff and experts can be accessed 24/7 via roaming robots or multi-function kiosks
- instant purchase for phones and accessories, virtual shopping baskets and pop station lockers to facilitate easy and instant transactions

The concept has received a 96% positive customer experience score and seen a 70% increase in footfall at Comcentre, with 30% operational savings.

EIGHT STEPS TO DELIVERING A SUCCESSFUL PHYSICAL AND VIRTUAL WORKPLACE EXPERIENCE

1 Be intentional

What is the goal? Who is the audience? How will the experience unfold? Where will it be? Serendipity can be built into an experience, for example by inviting a diverse group of people to come together for a common goal. But it should not be relied upon as the driver for delivering experiences. Great experiences that can be repeated and scaled need to be 'staged' according to Jim Gilmore, well planned and executed.

To develop a meaningful solution it is important to be clear about the problem to be solved as, to quote Peter F. Drucker, 'The most serious mistakes are not being made as a result of wrong answers. The true dangerous thing is asking the wrong question.'[5]

A good technique for getting to the heart of the problem is the 'Five Whys Method'. Sakichi Toyota, the Japanese industrialist, inventor, and founder of Toyota Industries, developed the Five Whys technique in the 1930s; it is a simple form of root-cause analysis.[6] The technique can be deployed to help uncover the potential outcome(s) of the experience when these are not immediately clear. In figure 5.03 (overleaf), the starting point is an ambiguous statement about creating spaces that help people to collaborate more when in the office. However, because collaboration is not an outcome in itself, asking 'Why?' five times over reveals that the intent of the experience was in fact to strengthen and grow social capital or trust within the team, by giving them the opportunity to connect and share personal information. An experience designed to deliver personal connections and trust will look and feel very different from one designed to promote collaboration.

2 Be authentic and unique

To achieve their intended purpose, workplace experiences need to link to the culture of the organisation hosting them; if not, they can feel forced. For example, an experience appropriate to a tech firm may not be right for a retail bank. Experiences should be based on everyday moments that can be redesigned and made into unique 'signature experiences', as described by Tim Greenhalgh of Landor & Fitch. As an example, the warm cookie given to guests when checking into a Hilton hotel is a gesture to reflect the warmth of hospitality. The experience is not just about getting the cookie, it is made personal by how the cookie is given – by a person with a smile, and as a replacement for the impersonal chocolate on a pillow.

3 Develop a new approach to workplace experience

When designing an office the experience has often been mapped by creating a 'day-in-the-life' scenario based on the 5E customer experience model (Entice, Enter, Engage, Exit, Extend).[7]

5E Model

1. **Entice:** how to capture someone's attention, i.e. what happens before they arrive at the building
2. **Enter:** the quality of the welcome as they enter
3. **Engage:** the touchpoints that occur when using the space
4. **Exit:** the farewell and departure experience
5. **Extend:** what it takes to keep people coming back for more

Now that the workplace ecosystem has evolved and the majority of people can choose where and when they work based on the task at hand, scenarios based on a typical day-in-the-life are no longer as effective.

Understanding personas, from visitor to senior manager, provides insight into the needs and motivations of different employee groups. This should be blended with

Figure 5.03: The 'Five Whys Method'

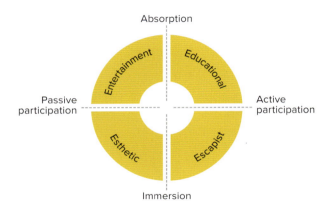

Figure 5.04: The 'Four Realms of an Experience' model by Pine and Gilmore is a framework for designing the new workplace experience typology.

the 'purpose' of the organisation when designing new workplace experience typologies to support increasingly diverse employee needs.

Blurring the lines between retail and work experiences, the digital bank Virgin Money has piloted how concepts from its high-street banks, called 'spaces', can inform its offices: see case study 5.03. The idea is to forge stronger alignment between the brand promise, the space and the newly introduced 'A Life More Virgin' principles, a values-led approach to flexible working.

CHAPTER 5: OPERATIONALISING THE WORKPLACE EXPERIENCE

CASE STUDY 5.03

VIRGIN MONEY'S *BIG RED BOOK*

LOCATION: GLOBAL

CONCEPT DESIGN: VIRGIN MONEY IN-HOUSE TEAMS

Virgin Money's upbeat high-street proposition is to provide spaces that enable customers to learn, work and play. They drive brand and behaviour, enabling staff to 'walk the talk' by working 'shoulder to shoulder' with customers rather than serving from behind a glass-fronted counter. The experience is characterised as open, feel-good, generous, optimistic and contemporary.

Designing and delivering the retail experience was a joint effort between the marketing and real estate teams. Virgin has created *The Big Red Book* as a guide to the in-store experience, not just to the space's design, but also to staff behaviour and how to tailor each experience to the location.

The customer journey is core to the experience and consists of a series of meaningful moments. 'It is these moments that make our experience unique. They are the moments in the customer journey where we can transform experiences through thoughtful and well-orchestrated brand interventions.' (*The Big Red Book*)

How people are placed in the space is vital

1. All staff rotate through all functions
2. Manager to ensure everything running smoothly
3. Look after your visitor from hello to goodbye

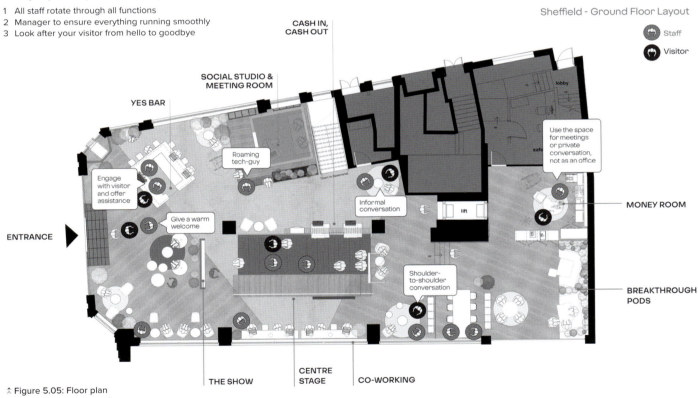

Figure 5.05: Floor plan illustrating the configuration of space and services

④ Take an integrated approach using holistic teams

For new workplace experiences to be successful they require an integrated strategy and delivery model where the business, human resources, real estate, occupier, landlord (where appropriate) and FM teams work together to design and deliver workplace solutions. How that experience is executed is as important as how it is conceptualised, therefore having teams with complementary but different expertise working together will improve outcomes. An integrated team would consider not only the design for the purpose of the experience, but also for its execution.

⑤ Think about making memories – the peak-end rule

The way an experience ends, positively or negatively, impacts people's recollections of the entire experience. Called the peak-end rule, this is a cognitive bias in how people remember past events. Intense positive or negative moments, the 'peaks', and the final moments of an experience, the 'end', are heavily weighted in our mental calculus.[8]

For example, an amazing holiday can be spoiled by an awful journey home. Conversely, a good ending can turn a bad situation around. This is a fundamental tenet in the hospitality industry; things will inevitably go wrong, but it is how they are dealt with and resolved that stands out in the memory.

⑥ Measure what matters, not just what's easy

Businesses are increasingly looking to make decisions based on workplace-experience data. Referring back to the workplace experience pyramid (figure 5.02), the 'functional' and contextual layers, which contribute to operational performance (everything from lighting and heating to water quality), can be measured using sensors and detectors.

Measuring the less tangible 'human' element of the experience is more difficult and is often limited to online employee surveys focused on gathering perception data. To add true value, the measurement criteria should be linked to the desired intent of the workplace experience and take into account any change that has occurred, as people tend to prefer what they know rather than something new.

For more rounded and predictive measures, perception data should be blended with sentiment analysis, also known as sentiment mining or emotional AI. This understands the voice of the employee by using natural-language processing (NLP) to analyse free-flow text. In its most basic form, it will classify text as positive or negative, but in more complex forms it is possible to start assigning meaning to data sets, giving insights into 'the why' that is driving 'the what'. Organisations should:

- **Take a strategic approach:** Start with the desired outcome and design a measurement strategy aligned to it.

- **Collect disconnected sources of data:** These can include sensor readings (occupancy; resource usage: coffee, soap dispensers, printing, food sales; ambient environmental readings: heat, light, temperature; plant, machinery and digital twins), qualitative data; employee feedback; pulse checks; engagement scores; net promoter scores including sentiment analysis; and sensory surveys.

- **Report insights not data:** Blend disconnected data to understand 'the what, the why and the so what'; avoid confirmation bias.

- **Action outcomes:** Many organisations have access to data, but don't have the ability outside of capital projects to action beneficial outcomes due to disconnected systems and processes leading to a lack of ownership and accountability.

7 **Build it and they will come ... but find out why**

The mechanics of the workplace experience, space and service, can 'nudge' desired behaviours, but they will not drive them. The 'humanics' or human side of the experience needs to be led with a hospitality, not an operational, mindset. The experience should centre around what the employees actually need and value, and not just what has traditionally been supplied.

8 **Ensure every workplace experience is a tailored solution**

In a hybrid model, the workplace is anywhere that workers choose and is not limited to the office. Therefore, when curating workplace experiences they should embrace an ecosystem of places both physical and virtual. The 'follow me' concept allows people to roam freely across their workplace ecosystem for an equitable experience.

The array of workplace experiences on offer needs to reflect hybrid-working policies and an organisation's duty of care. How is the experience equitable across the ecosystem considering the diversity of employees, their needs and their motivations to work? How should it cater for workers who don't keep standard hours?

SHIFTING TO EQUITABLE WORKPLACE EXPERIENCES

Times are changing. The main challenges organisations face in providing an array of equitable workplace experiences are now being addressed:

- **Moving from the traditional focus on operational excellence:** Facilities management has traditionally followed the mindset of, and recruited from, the logistics areas of the armed services, where operational excellence is key. However, a hospitality mindset is required to elevate and curate the workplace experience. Service providers should look to the hotel industry for ideas regarding processes, recruitment and training.

- **Efficiencies or effectiveness as pointers to success:** Traditionally, real estate and facilities management functions report to the COO/CFO, making efficiencies not effectiveness the main measure of success. Recent shifts have seen workplace managers starting to report to HR, a positive move for improving the link between people, purpose and place.

- **Experience is personal:** Office space and service was traditionally designed and deployed for an unspecified 'standard' worker. Recognising the importance of supporting the diversity and inclusion of workers, experience design should follow a mass-customisation model enabling an equitable array of workplace experiences.

CASE STUDY 5.04

Jaego's House

LOCATION: LONDON, UK
DELIVERY: LITTLE HOUSES GROUP
COMPLETION: 2022

Jaego's House is a community hub in north London, accessible to all — a place that brings people together to enjoy quality time with family and friends. By combining co-working with childcare, the club caters for remote-working parents by providing a space where they can work with their pre-school children on site rather than having to drop them off at a separate crèche or nursery. In a post-Covid-19 world, where hybrid working is here to stay and the purpose of the office is evolving, a space where families can work, rest and play together under one roof is an innovative idea that fills a gap in the market.

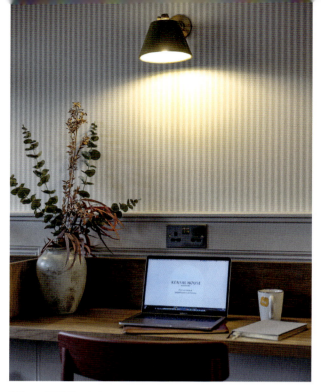

↑ Figure 5.07: Touch-down workstations available for use

↞ Figure 5.06: The spin studio at Jaego's House

↑ Figure 5.08: A soft play space for children

CHAPTER 5: OPERATIONALISING THE WORKPLACE EXPERIENCE

CASE STUDY 5.05
Hines – Grainhouse

LOCATION: LONDON, UK

ARCHITECT: BARR GAZETAS

DEVELOPER: HINES

COMPLETION: 2023

Global real estate investment, development and property manager Hines has selected the London cultural destination Drury Lane in Covent Garden as the location for its new UK and European headquarters. The heritage-led regeneration, acquired on behalf of the Hines European Value Fund 2 (HEVF 2) in 2020, consolidates five eclectic buildings, including a nineteenth-century chapel and a twentieth-century grain store, into one cutting-edge workplace. Office workers will benefit from easy access to the surrounding cafes, restaurants, theatres and museums, as well as the 2,043 square metres of retail and amenities, based mostly on the ground floor of Grainhouse. Hines envisages attracting a range of tenants — such as a gym, bars and cafes which will spill out onto a newly pedestrianised street with outdoor dining — offering a dynamic and self-sustaining workplace for users.

Figure 5.09: Ground-level retail units will be open to the public, creating a dynamic and amenity-rich place of work for Hines employees and other occupiers.

Figure 5.10: Hines have been granted planning permission to pedestrianise one of the streets Grainhouse faces — creating a lively streetscape.

CONCLUSION

Because many workers today are able to choose when and where they work, they base their decisions on personal preference ahead of business needs. Workplace experiences must provide equitable outcomes regardless of being physical, virtual, at home or in the office. Experiences need to be customisable to individuals or groups working together, to prevent high levels of customer 'sacrifice' – settling for what there is, not what is wanted, needed or valued. When choosing where to work, the return on investment of time and resource is a key factor; a good experience will make the effort worthwhile.

For a hybrid workforce, that experience needs to offer something they value that they cannot get when working elsewhere: peace and quiet, access to equipment, the ability to meet and work with colleagues face-to-face, a unique learning opportunity, the ability to improve well-being, or a post-work activity.

The consumerisation of the workplace continues to follow the trends seen in our personal lives, with super apps playing a key role in collating and delivering frictionless work experiences. Apps need careful content curation and should not replace the human touchpoints that provide personalisation.

Organisations need to be able to measure current – and predict future – workplace experiences to understand how to invest and how to allocate resources appropriately. There should be a clear measure of success (desired outcome) to create experiences that will deliver success and value. To do this effectively it is important to understand an array of employee personas, as well as what people value and are motivated by at work.

Traditional archetypes of work should be challenged and redesigned to better align with the desired experience. For example, should the reception space and experience be dedicated to monitoring and assisting ease of access into the building? Handing out security passes? Or could it be redesigned and curated to provide a meaningful 'peak' moment of connecting and welcoming employees to the company space and culture?

When experiences are rich and varied, authentic and human, workers are most likely to invest time in their commute and feel positive about their workplace. Jaego's House is a new kind of private family members' club created by Charlie Gardiner, founder of Incipio Group, which challenges the typical archetype of the workplace experience.

LEARNING POINTS

- The currency of experience is time.
- Services are delivered; experiences are curated.
- Start with the intent in mind, consider the desired effect of the experience and curate and activate the outcome.
- Workplace experience should be data-driven and insight-led.
- Memorable experiences need to be tailored to personal preferences and have a positive impact.

- Space and service can act as a tangible nudge, but people and interaction will drive experience; therefore, while operational excellence is a given, lead with a hospitality mindset.
- Workplace experience blurs the boundaries and requires integrated input from service partners, facilities management, real estate, human resources, IT and business representatives.

- Fresh eyes are required to curate workplace experiences for hybrid working. The focus should be on doing it the best way, not just the way we have always done it.
- Hybrid-working policies require 'follow me' tailored workplace experience solutions.
- The experience needs to be enticing to get people to join and compelling to get them to return – don't underestimate the power of delight and surprise.

CHAPTER 6

The value and purpose of place

INTRODUCTION

Value and place have always been closely connected. In 1944, when asked to name three things that mattered in real estate, Landsec founder Harold Samuel coined the phrase, 'location, location, location'. This emphatic response underscored a simple truth: *where* an asset is located has a significant bearing on its value.

Almost a century on and the value and purpose of real estate and place are undergoing significant reappraisal. Laid bare by the Covid-19 pandemic, drivers such as globalisation, automation and digitalisation threaten to unseat long-established principles, as the workplace and workers' needs evolve.

It is difficult to imagine what Samuel and his colleagues would make of the recent ventures into virtual locations. In February 2022, an investor parted with $450,000 for a parcel of virtual real estate located next door to rapper Snoop Dog in the metaverse.[1] Time and context have moved on, but it seems that location still matters. Nevertheless, as the essence of location grows in complexity, we are uncovering new truths around the purpose and value of place.

WHY DOES PLACE HAVE VALUE?

At its simplest, real estate value is a function of supply and demand. Compared with other assets, land has an advantage in that supply is finite. As Mark Twain once said, 'Buy land; they're not making it anymore.' Focus then shifts to demand, which is more complex.

Demand for land and buildings comes from the opportunities they provide for pursuing personal and commercial activities. As an illustration, few people choose to live or work in remote locations such as Greenland, Mongolia or Eastern Siberia. Consequently, land in these places has low value. In the case of the latter, the Russian government has in fact been prepared to give it away for free, or even with incentives, for those who are willing to make a go of it.[2]

Through the ages, the value of most land was measured simply. Demand, and hence value, was highest in areas that provided natural advantages. For early man, access to natural resources such as drinking water, river transport and prey was critical. A secondary factor was the ability to defend this land against others, and so topography was also important. Most of the major cities around the world were developed where these factors were combined.

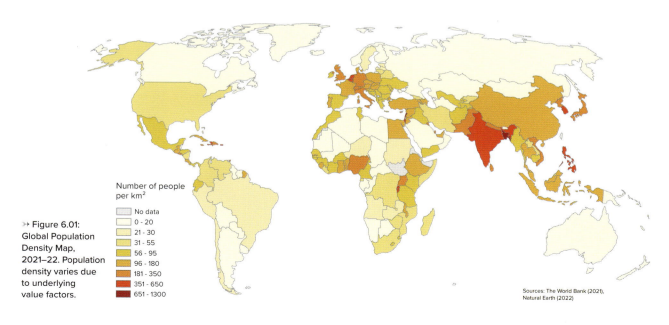

↳ Figure 6.01: Global Population Density Map, 2021–22. Population density varies due to underlying value factors.

Sources: The World Bank (2021), Natural Earth (2022)

Demand is not a binary function; some land offers the opportunity to carry out activities in a way that is more valuable to the user, and this is reflected in a sliding scale of price. For most of human history, our economy has been based on agriculture. Hence the strength of the economy was a function of the productivity or yield of the fields, and our ability to commercialise this. Therefore, the highest demand would be for fields that were naturally fertile and so likely to produce a stronger harvest. It also stands to reason that there would be higher demand for fields that were closer to a marketplace, because proximity confers a commercial advantage.

DEMAND AND THE THEORY OF RENT

Eighteenth-century economist David Ricardo developed this thinking into his 'Theory of Rent',[3] which has been subsequently developed in a modern context into 'bid rent theory'.[4] The logic was founded on an assumption that in a competitive market, land value is an 'economic residual'. Otherwise put, the value of the land is what is left over once the costs of the operation carried out on it have been subtracted from the value of these operations. So, in the case of our field the cost of operations is largely the cost of labour and the cost of transporting the goods to market, whereas the value of the operations is the amount that the crop can be sold for at the market. It follows that a field that is further away from the market will attract a lower rent than a field that is near the market and hence requires lower transportation costs. Location, location, location.

This is the most important principle in defining the financial value of place – it is an eternal truth. However, fields are much less relevant to the modern context. As our economy has grown in complexity and value, and become first industrial and now service-led, new value drivers have come into play. Many of these now concern the value of being near other people, rather than near natural resources.

AMENITY, AGGLOMERATION AND SERENDIPITY

People derive value and purpose from location in three principal ways: amenity, agglomeration and serendipity.

	AMENITY	AGGLOMERATION	SERENDIPITY
What?	A thing	An ecosystem	An event
Example	A park	A shopping centre	A chance encounter
Value exchange	Bilateral	Multilateral	Bilateral
Predictability	Certain	Strong	Uncertain
Activity	I travel there	I travel within it	It happens when I'm there
Interaction	Planned	Planned	Unplanned
Relies on …	Quality / proximity	Scale / commonality	Frequency / uniqueness

Table 6.01: The three vehicles through which value is derived from place, and their differences

Figure 6.02: All other factors being equal, fields closer to the marketplace command a higher rent.

Amenity

In the same way that the farmer found benefit in being near the marketplace, so modern urbanites find value in being close to a broader collection of amenities. It adds convenience to life to be within walking distance of a shop. It also adds value to life to be near a park or a beautiful view. Because these amenities are scarce, there is clear evidence that people are willing to pay more to live close to them.[5,6]

Agglomeration

This is more complex than amenity. Whereas amenities like parks tend to be intransigent, agglomerations are dependent on more precarious ecosystems and symbioses. Agglomerations tend to start with one leader. In days gone by this might have been the king. Wherever the king set up court, an ecosystem of commerce sprung up around him. A more recent example would be that high-street shops have been attracted to pitches around major department stores. The sustainability of demand, however, comes not from a single operator, but from the total ecosystem. The more shops there are, the more likely it is that this critical mass attracts the customers upon which the ecosystem thrives. Some agglomerations can be quite specific. For instance, London's Hatton Garden is known as a place to buy jewellery. It is the informal ties of commercially aligned businesses that create common identity and serve as the glue for these ecosystems.

In the workplace context, agglomerations succeed because they provide efficient interactions through the co-location of collaborators and supply chain, and they create a magnet for talent, which creates deeper and more predictable labour markets. Silicon Valley originally formed due to the presence of a natural amenity (silicon); however, it remains successful because it has developed into an agglomeration for the tech sector and a predictable talent pool.

Serendipity

The least predictable and the most exciting of these values. Sometimes, the most amazing things happen by accident. This could be the chance conversation that unlocks a business opportunity, or the collision with a stranger on the street that eventually leads to marriage. By definition, these things cannot be planned or orchestrated; however, it is possible to influence their likelihood. Consider your high-school chemistry class on rates of reaction — the collision frequency of particles depends on temperature and density. The more particles there are within a confined space, the higher the likelihood of their collision.

Cities and workplaces follow these same principles. The higher the number of participants in a system of fixed dimensions, the more likely it is that collisions will occur. And the higher the number of collisions, the more likely it is that one of them will create something valuable. So when we come into the office, the most valuable conversations often result from the surprise collision consequent on putting many people in the same space. This, perhaps more than other factors, points to the most valuable purpose of the office of the future.

◂◂ Figure 6.03: London's historic jewellery quarter Hatton Garden remains home to over 50 jewellery shops.

CASE STUDY 6.01
Location Strategy Trends

LOCATION: GLOBAL

As location becomes a broader and more complex concept, corporate real estate portfolio strategy at a city and global level is shifting from a centralised model to a more distributed, on-demand space provision that provides flexibility and fluidity. With proximity to the office becoming less important, companies are shifting to global talent-sourcing strategies and are expanding to regional cities that offer access to good universities and a combination of affordability and higher quality of life. Metrics such as cost of living, cultural vibrancy, climate conditions and public-transit infrastructure are becoming more important in location selection. For example, Meta will open its first European Meta Lab for remote workers in Madrid, with a plan to hire up to 2,000 people over the next five years, while Accenture India has relocated to tier 2 cities, such as Jaipur and Coimbatore, as part of a move to access more talent and give employees greater flexibility of workplace.

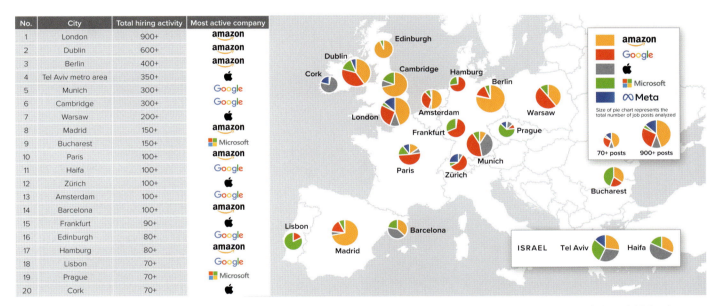

Figure 6.04: London, Dublin and Berlin are the hottest markets for big tech hires.

Figure 6.05: Top 25 tech investment destinations in Europe based on volume of Foreign Direct Investment

MODERN VALUE MODELS

As urban environments have become more complex, the calculation of value has also become more challenging. Nevertheless, the general rule holds true that the most valuable land and the highest rents in a city tend to be in the centre. This is where demand for a range of different activities (shopping, working, leisure and living) is predictably highest. It is where there is the greatest evel of commercial and cultural amenity. It is where the highest value agglomerations exist, and it offers the highest probability of valuable serendipity.

Moving out from the city centre, distance is now less important than time. We no longer travel on straight roads to marketplaces. In large cities, many of us travel on public transport, and so accessibility is more important than linear distance. In an unpublished study conducted by Cushman & Wakefield in 2022, it was found that for London's residential flats, there is a 70% correlation between time to a notional 'centre' and the per-square-metre value of flatted accommodation.[7] Hence, when new infrastructure is developed that reduces time to the centre, local real estate markets shoot up in value.

The second big factor affecting value is scale. It makes sense that the more accommodation that can be squeezed on the same plot, the more valuable will be the underlying land. There tends also to be a covariance of location with scale, in that the tallest buildings in a city are often (but not always) found in the centre. This reinforces the value of central real estate.

The third factor is found in permitted use. Until relatively recently, as a landowner, it was possible to build whatever you wanted on your land. The arrival of planning controls now fetters this ability. While optimising the economic and social value for all of society, these controls restrict the private financial value for the landowner. For instance, the highest rents for industrial space in the UK are roughly 20% of the value of equivalently sized office space. Other planning mechanisms, such as sequential testing and public transport accessibility level (PTAL) ratings, again reinforce the dominance and value of central real estate.

It may be an uncomfortable truth for designers that location, massing and permitted use are much bigger drivers of value than design. The difference between the top and bottom rent of new Grade A office buildings in the City of London is relatively small. The value is principally set before the designing commences.

In turn, these value and cost factors influence the make-up of cities. Centrally located areas of high-value amenity, such as Kensington or the Upper East Side, are mostly the domain of the rich. Meanwhile, high streets are dominated by chain stores that have the greatest efficiencies and can afford to offer the highest rents.

Will this remain the case? Fundamental forces are reshaping our cities. Particularly, the internet, automation, rapid transit, globalisation and new ways of working, shopping and living are undermining the biggest driver of the value of place — its location. In this new world, does place still matter? And what new factors are emerging that might have a greater bearing on value?

CHAPTER 6: THE VALUE AND PURPOSE OF PLACE

CASE STUDY 6.02

Battersea Power Station

LOCATION: LONDON, UK

LEAD ARCHITECT: WILKINSONEYRE

DEVELOPER: BATTERSEA POWER STATION DEVELOPMENT COMPANY

COMPLETION: 2022

Standing on the banks of the River Thames on the edge of central London, Battersea Power Station is one of the best-known landmarks in the UK. Like many early power stations, its location was selected at a site close to the consumers of power, and also close to a functional amenity – the cooling waters of the Thames.

As the national model for power production changed, the power station became obsolete, leaving the 17-hectare (42-acre) site needing a new use. Since it was decommissioned in 1983, a

6.06: Battersea Power Station has long been an icon of the London skyline.

Figure 6.07: Battersea Power Station, 2022 – a place for living, working and relaxing

93

↑ Figure 6.08: Although repurposed, it remains recognisable as the power station.

variety of proposals were brought (including a theme park); none of these progressed.[8] From 2012, a series of factors which illustrate some of the themes of this chapter conspired to bring forward the development of the site under new ownership.

Approved in 2014, the introduction of a new piece of infrastructure, the Northern Line extension, unlocked connectivity to the heart of London, reducing the journey time to the West End to under 10 minutes, and essentially bringing the site into the central zone. Rail accessibility, in turn, allowed for the density and heights of the site to be expanded in common with neighbouring sites, which improved the underlying land value.

Meanwhile, in 2015 the relocation of the US Embassy to nearby Nine Elms created confidence in the location, acting as an anchor for an agglomeration of other commercial activities on previously industrial land.[9] This unlocked the viability of a range of more valuable uses, which allowed the developers to tap into London's booming residential market and provide a new retail agglomeration to service a rapidly growing catchment.

As the site was developed, close attention was paid to establishing the brand of the location, drawing strong symbolism from the pedigree of the iconic structures on the site, as well as developing a fresh and challenging identity compared with more established locations.[10] This was achieved through a mix of 'meanwhile uses', such as Red Bull, actively using the heritage assets as part of the scheme proposition rather than treating them as a barrier, and securing a critical mass of exciting office and retail occupiers such as Apple and IWG, which created a sustainable and mutually reinforcing ecosystem.

The scheme, which was substantially launched in 2022, serves as a strong example of placemaking, and the value of creating mixed-use agglomerations around a common and well-defined sense of identity.

A NEW PURPOSE FOR PLACE

The role of place has evolved and grown in complexity throughout history. It began as somewhere with access to natural resources, and protection from the elements and from others. As the global economy has matured, so place has found new meaning as somewhere that enables productivity, to harvest more crops or benefit from business interactions. As these factors become commoditised, place once again needs to rise up the value curve.

Chapter 3 draws from Maslow's works on the hierarchy of human needs. The basics of physiological and security needs have largely been achieved for most in the West; thankfully few people are homeless, and workplaces have become safe, climate-controlled environments. To continue to add value, therefore, place has increasingly shifted its focus to service higher-order purposes, such as the need for belonging and the opportunity to live one's fullest life.

This starts with aspirational buildings where, for example, people feel proud to work. It includes experiential retail offerings where people can find something unique and entertaining to talk about with their friends. It also now includes 'Instagrammable' locations, which allow people to not only enjoy an interesting activity, but to document and share that experience in a way that establishes personal social worth.[11,12] In a world where most functional activities can now be done from home, the purpose of central places is increasingly as an access point to rarefied and higher-value activities.

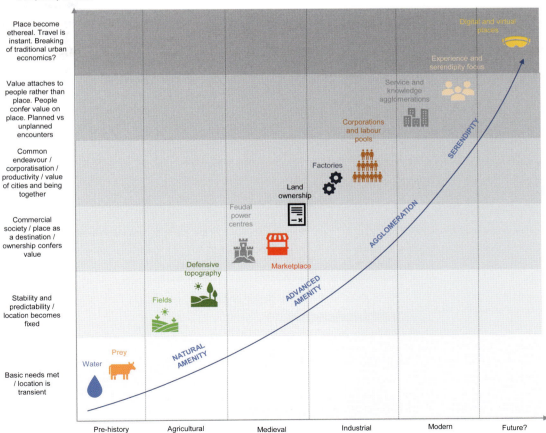

Figure 6.09: Evolving value drivers of place – from a focus on natural amenities towards the value of human interaction

These factors have been thrown into sharper relief by the post-pandemic work-model shift. As discussed in chapters 1 and 2, the majority of white-collar workers now have a degree of personal choice to work at least part of the week at home. In this context, the benefits of coming into the office (connection/collaboration/social elements of work) are being actively weighed by these workers against the personal drawbacks of doing so (commuting/ privacy/loss of free time). Particularly, post-pandemic survey evidence points to *connection* as the biggest driver for choosing the office as a place to work.[13] Primarily this is connection with colleagues; however, it is also connection with corporate culture, both of which have waned as hybrid and remote working have increased.

It is serendipity in particular that suffers in a more remote work model; the chance encounter that unlocks a profit opportunity, or the overheard conversation that leads to learning and career development. More than ever, serendipity now sits at the centre of the purpose of place, as factors of amenity and agglomeration can now be synthesised at home through digital means.

Connections also breed culture, which in turn drives corporate and brand loyalty.[14] Place is often the physical manifestation of a company. The headquarters of an investment bank speaks to the success, solvency and provenance of its business, whereas a showcase store creates a direct conversation between retailers and customers around the lifestyle values of their products. As functional, commoditised activities are stripped out of place, so the void is filled with a greater emphasis on brand value, customer creation and employee attraction.

These factors themselves are also shifting quickly. Today, a company's brand is highly shaped by its reputation on what is now a balanced scorecard of ESG factors, rather than by a narrow lens on financial performance. Workers are seeking jobs which provide a social purpose rather than just a paycheque. Similarly, consumers are buying products which speak to their ethical values rather than just performing functional requirements. If it is the purpose of place to respond to these factors, then how we design and manage our buildings must inevitably change.

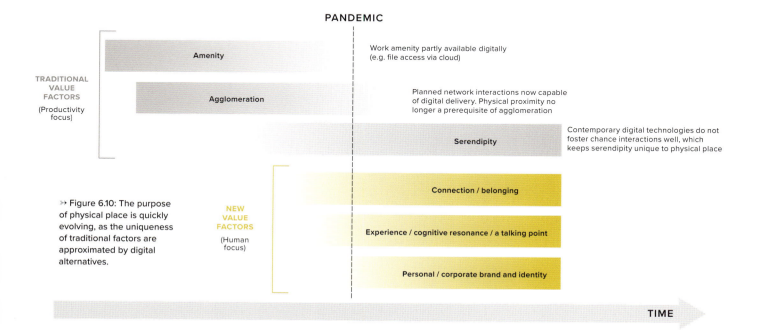

➤ Figure 6.10: The purpose of physical place is quickly evolving, as the uniqueness of traditional factors are approximated by digital alternatives.

These elements of the corporate value chain are a world away from being somewhere to execute tasks, and their worth cannot be sensibly judged against historic utilisation or productivity metrics. In this context, office investors should anticipate that the willingness of occupiers to pay rent will over time drift towards buildings that satisfy these new requirements. Objectively well-located and functionally utilitarian floor plates will give way to interesting, nuanced structures that in equal measure speak to company values and excite workers. The success of aligning to this new purpose will be a central determinant of future value.

CASE STUDY 6.03
Walt Disney World Resort

LOCATION: ORLANDO, FLORIDA, USA

Few other places on earth have the same intense focus on placemaking as Disney World. Every year over 50 million people visit the 10,117-hectare (25,000-acre) theme park in Florida, which as recently as 1970 was an unused swamp.[15] How did Disney create one of the world's most valuable locations?

In 1971 when the park was opened, Disney already had a well-established brand and experience of running a theme park in California. This brand, which today is ranked in the top 10 most valuable in the world, is inextricably linked with the physical place and confers value upon the park.[16]

Walt Disney World is the biggest theme park in the world and contains almost 200 rides across seven individually themed domains. The scale of the agglomeration is unique and creates a destination for those looking to experience many attractions in one visit. The theming is meticulous and confers a defined sense of place to each of the parks individually and in totality.

By seeding an agglomeration that people wanted to visit, Disney created an epicentre of value that ripples outwards. It had achieved the same previously in California, and others had profited from Disney's investment by developing hotels and other attractions on the periphery. When developing Florida, Disney purchased surrounding land before opening the park, over time allowing it to develop its own hotels and retail offering to capture the created value.[17]

Figure 6.11: Disney's Magic Kingdom Park, Florida

As we have moved into the digital age, Disney has been unafraid to pioneer and develop its own digital proposition. The operations of the park are now highly digitalised, oriented around an app and a $1 billion investment in its MagicBand technology.[18] This seamlessly blends the online and offline experience, helping to reduce queuing times, facilitating purchases and supporting the delivery of a more personalised experience.

Meanwhile, Disney has also embraced virtual technologies in delivering its rides. A modern breed of attractions, such as Avatar and Star Wars: Galaxy's Edge, allows visitors to experience a blend of actual and virtual reality in the same ride. The physical place creates the anticipation and interactions and houses the expensive hardware; the virtual technologies add sparkle to the experience not possible in the real world.

Above all, Disney focuses on creating places where people want to be. Its mission, 'to entertain, inform and inspire', translates to its physical places and responds to the emerging role and purpose of a much broader category of places, including the workplace. Although workplace managers will not have the same enviable budget to invest in place, much can be gained through adopting similar value drivers.

CONCLUSION

As we enter a period of rapid digitalisation and virtualisation, many parallels can be drawn between the fundamental principles and evolution of physical places and their virtual equivalents. Simplistically, successful digital places are also ones which drive amenity, agglomeration and serendipity.

Consider a social media platform. The platform itself needs to offer a slick user experience that creates a functional amenity for users. However, its most valuable function comes from having attracted other users and content contributors that create value for each other through network effects. Often, this is through defined networks and agglomerations (such as your friends on Facebook). In other cases, it is serendipitous and random encounters with new content that provokes novel thinking (for instance TikTok's 'For You' page). The place/location/platform where most people congregate, and hence where demand is focused, carries the most value.

As the interactive sophistication of these platforms increases, for example as metaverses gain traction, it is only a matter of time before digital and physical places will be competing for the same spend, by aiming to be the best places to deliver commercial and social amenity. In this context, physical place will need to work increasingly hard to stay in front. Chapter 9 develops this idea further.

LEARNING POINTS

- Real estate value is a function of supply and demand. Land has finite supply. Demand is unequally distributed. For some land, demand is so low that it is essentially valueless, whereas we see significant spikes in demand in major cities.

- Historically, demand (hence value) was focused on places of natural amenity (rivers, fertile fields), and places of societal advantage (defensible hilltops). Contours of value rippled out from epicentres of activity, creating a premium for being close to the centre.

- Historically, the location of a property has been the most significant determinant of value. The ability to build at different heights combined with modern restrictions on use now provide a more complex construct of value.

- People derive value from place in three principal forms: amenity – the conferral of a functional benefit; agglomeration – the value of being part of an ecosystem of actors; and serendipity – the value of chance encounters.

- The purpose of place is evolving. As functional activities are increasingly automated, delivered through digital means, or delivered in de-central locations, the role of central real estate is increasingly focusing on higher-value activities.

- The purpose of central places is increasingly about connectivity (to others and to companies) and social fulfilment. These have been thrown in sharp relief by the post-pandemic work model shift.

- Many factors that drive value in physical place also drive value for digital places. Physical place should exploit its inherent advantage over digital places; however, the gap is closing as digital worlds continue to evolve.

CHAPTER 7

Experience destinations

INTRODUCTION

Recognising that workers will come to the office for significant events, collaboration with colleagues and social gatherings, a high-quality, tailored experience is at the core of making those visits worthwhile, productive, even essential.

As explored in chapters 5 and 6, much has been learned from the retail, leisure and hospitality sectors about the ingredients that make positive experiences. They offer physical connections, enjoyment and stimulation, delight and surprise, along with reinforcing 'tribe' and brand loyalty.

And experience is not just about physical place – it is holistic, a multi-platform phenomenon involving a location or an event (such as the Olympic Games). This chapter provides a showcase of different types of destinations where the experience has been intentionally designed.

WHY EXPERIENCE MATTERS

In both the physical and virtual workplace, the quality of experience underpins why workers remain productive, active and loyal. While people remain the largest cost to an organisation, the business of attracting and retaining them and ensuring they are productive is critical to financial success.

Experiences provide humans with intrinsic benefits; they leave an imprint in the form of memories which stay with us, guide us and grow over time. Negative experiences may make us wary and unwilling to return. Good experiences leave us feeling positive and craving more. Experiences inform our beliefs which, in turn, influence actions and behaviours.

As explored in chapter 5 (page 76), an experience can be defined as 'the aggregated touchpoints connecting people, purpose, and place'. This is about creating memorable moments and, when applied to the workplace, the desired outcome. This may be to provide time saved, where the participant benefits from the efficiency of the experience, or time well spent, where the participant benefits from the effectiveness of the experience by learning, connecting to information and to people. Now that people have choice, the perceived experience of an organisation is a fundamental factor in deciding where to work.

Providing a diverse workplace ecosystem is no longer enough. To make places successful organisations must integrate intentional, authentic, multidisciplinary experiences with data-driven, hospitality-minded implementation.

We define experience destinations as places that create – and leave – a positive memory with the visitor. As an example, the Brent Cross Town development in London (case study 7.01) places health, fitness and well-being at the heart of its concept.

CASE STUDY 7.01

Brent Cross Town

LOCATION: BRENT CROSS, LONDON, UK

DEVELOPERS: RELATED ARGENT WITH BARNET COUNCIL

COMPLETION: ONGOING

Health and wellness, social connectivity and sustainability are values at the heart of a mixed-use development underway in north west London. Called Brent Cross Town (BXT), this reworking of 73 hectares of land will include 6,700 homes, workplaces for 25,000 people in up to 280,000 square metres of offices, as well as schools and shops, all set around more than 20 hectares of parks, playing fields and state-of-the-art sporting facilities. A new rail station will connect the scheme to central London within 12 minutes, and climate change is being addressed by achieving net zero carbon by 2030 at the latest.

Central to the wider plan is Project Play, designed for the playing fields in the south of the scheme. The vision is to use sports and play to 'transform lives, unite people and build communities,' by putting health, fitness and well-being at the heart of the town.[1] In time the multi-sport and play offering on the playing fields will be supplemented by indoor sport facilities.

The appeal is for all ages and all capabilities, with most facilities on the playing fields offered for free. Outdoor activities in the parks and playing fields will enable everyone to enjoy traditional sports such as football, hockey and netball; challenger sports such as skateboarding, BMX, bouldering and parkour; and social sports that include pickleball, teqball, table tennis and boule. Also planned are outdoor gyms, weekly park runs and lots of open spaces to relax and just play.

Figure 7.01: Brent Cross Town masterplan – illustrating the clear prioritisation of green space

Figure 7.02: Walking routes will be signposted to encourage people to explore the full extent of the area.

101

In addition to providing great amenities for residents, the parks and playing fields are also intended to support the new business community at BXT. There is a fundamental underlying belief that quality of life is the future of work and that offering people access to regular outdoor activities in a natural setting will attract and retain talent and improve their overall health and well-being. It is this offer that attracted Sheffield Hallam University to open a campus at BXT, becoming a key anchor tenant of the new town.

BXT draws on the '15-minute town' concept, where accessibility and walkability are priorities. Buildings are designed in conjunction with public spaces to create a seamless indoor-outdoor experience for lively and safe streets. The commercial district will support start-ups, corporates and academic institutions to help foster a strong community with shared values.

We have a great opportunity to invest in 20 hectares of green space and create a new kind of park that's never been seen in London before. We want to build a compelling mix of traditional sports like tennis, netball and football, alongside fun facilities such as bouldering and parkour, and social sports like boule and table tennis. We will reach across the boundaries of age and culture, empower female participation and champion inclusion and diversity.

MORWENNA HALL, PARTNER FOR RELATED ARGENT

Figure 7.03: Kids on a cycling proficiency course at Coal Drops Yard, King's Cross (delivered by Argent)

WHY AN EXPERIENCE DESTINATION?

To maximise their appeal, places need to have a clearly defined purpose. A single office location can accommodate numerous types of settings – sparking creativity and productivity. By contrast, working at home can be a single homogenous experience. But without a workplace focused on creating an immersive experience destination, we might as well stay at home.

Creating destinations with purpose requires the development to connect with the surrounding environment. A cohesive experience open to outside interactions acts as an attraction point in the urban landscape, pulling in neighbours directly adjacent and from further afield.

These elements, physical accessibility and permeability, are facilitated by visually connected lines of sight. In establishing a destination, an organisation needs to think about ways of tangibly giving back – not just investing in its employees, but also looking at how to invest in the community within which it is based. In its recent headquarters project, Ireland's Electricity Supply Board demonstrates its intent to be a good neighbour and an open resource; see case study 7.02.

One exemplar of creating an experience that embodies an organisation's values in a physical place is the new north of England home of the Royal College of Physicians, where wellness is a priority; see case study 7.03.

CASE STUDY 7.02

Electricity Supply Board Headquarters

LOCATION: DUBLIN, IRELAND

ARCHITECTS: GRAFTON ARCHITECTS AND O'MAHONY PIKE ARCHITECTS

INTERIOR DESIGN: AECOM

COMPLETION: 2021

Inspired by the history of its site and its surroundings, the new headquarters of the Energy Supply Board (ESB) was conceived as an accessible mixed-use scheme. A gradient of scaled experiences begins with the approach to the building and is used to highlight the wide variety of considerations that have been made for employees and neighbours.

As Ireland's largest utilities company, the state-owned ESB has set the ambitious target of reaching net zero carbon by 2040. This involves pivoting away from fossil-fuel-reliant energy production to more sustainable alternatives. The redevelopment of ESB's headquarters provided an opportunity to demonstrate the company's commitment to a low-carbon future, with sustainability designed into every aspect of this award-winning office development, benefiting workplace users and the surrounding neighbourhood.

Figure 7.04: A street view, replicating the granular flow of surrounding Georgian architecture

Architecture and user design

The new headquarters city block, by Grafton Architects and O'Mahony Pike Architects, comprises two interconnecting buildings with a new linking path. The facade is designed as a modern interpretation and continuation of the longest Georgian street in Europe.

The buildings offer opportunities to enhance worker well-being throughout the day. A sunken garden is a focal point – bringing light from above to the lower-ground amenity space. Two large roof terraces offer a place to work, relax and enjoy panoramic views. Throughout the building, interconnecting indoor-outdoor bridges enable people to move across floors and buildings with ease, benefiting from the movement and fresh air. The workspace has sit/standing desks and a variety of settings to suit users' changing work activity across the day.

Figure 7.05: ESB's headquarters prioritised a permeable ground-floor level.

Figure 7.06: The canteen provides an informal but dynamic space for socialising.

Figure 7.07: The reception area embodies ESB's brand and welcomes people with coffee from a repurposed yellow van.

An accessible mixed-use scheme

Public accessibility and permeability were key to the design. The footpath provides pedestrians with a route to a newly created public plaza – softening boundaries and creating a new public realm. The ground floor is part occupied by retail and food outlets, inviting public use with a more engaging streetscape. The development also includes a number of residential family units that have been sold to foster a stronger sense of community and to bring families back into the city.

Integrated approach to sustainability

A holistic approach to sustainability has helped this development use 52% less carbon than traditional office buildings and achieve a BREEAM Excellent certificate.

Sustainable design features include:

- a hybrid ventilation system, combining natural and mechanical conditioning
- ground- and air-source heat pumps for heating and cooling
- 200 square metres of solar panelling on the roof to generate clean energy
- rain- and well-water collection and reuse
- use of recycled materials from the previous building – the granite cladding is now the paving for the courtyard
- planting of the courtyard and roof terraces with drought-resistant plants, plus beehives for urban biodiversity

Energy use and waste are kept to the minimum through:

- low-water-use sanitary fittings (e.g. spray taps) which contribute a 70% reduction in water wastage
- single-temperature showers
- new comfort-control techniques to adjust heating and cooling
- installation of EV charging, electric cycle provision and a cycle-to-work scheme
- a 'no single-use plastics' policy
- a dedicated waste-management area.

Figure 7.08 (top): Design elements are used as visual cues to define spatial boundaries.

Figure 7.09: Planting on ESB's rooftop terrace is designed to encourage bees and contribute to local biodiversity.

KEY PRINCIPLES OF EXPERIENCE DESTINATIONS

The following principles outline key considerations when designing an experience destination. For employers, these are the elements that will connect an organisation to its urban context and signal to employees what it cares about most.

- **Strong brand vision:** Understanding and capturing what a brand stands for is the first step in developing a transformative experience. Brand principles should be woven through every part of the experience to evoke its story. This includes design, materials, acoustics and lighting, through to the approach to sustainability and customer care.

- **Location:** Whether the choice is between being a pioneer in a new development or seeking the reassurance of a historic setting, the location speaks volumes about what might be expected from the experience.

- **Getting there:** How people travel to, access and arrive at their destination will influence their experience.

- **Physical presence:** Everyone has the ability to 'read' a building and its environs. Experience tells us when a place is safe or edgy, when buildings are constructed to high standards or on a low budget, whether a place is oppressive and closed or positive, generous and uplifting.

- **Permeability:** Open and accessible ground floors along with a welcoming arrival experience create a sense of belonging, which is a social currency that strengthens the perceived experience of the destination.

- **Materiality:** Even though it may be subconscious, people have a sophisticated understanding of materials – not just in the way they look, but also how they feel. High-quality materials enrich experience. The full experience is determined by how the materials are deployed, finished, lit and maintained.

- **Immersive:** Successful destinations engage all five senses in positive and enjoyable ways. Using sight, sound, smell, touch and taste, high-quality shared experiences communicate group values.

- **Framed moments:** Whether tangible or intangible, a successful experience needs a memento. For an Instagram and TikTok generation, this can be a framed selfie opportunity. It evokes an emotion people will associate with the brand.

- **Strong ending:** Chapter 5 discussed the 'peak-end rule' which states that we all have cognitive bias that impacts how we remember past events. Intense positive or negative moments (peaks) and the final moments of an experience (end) are heavily weighted when storing memories (see page 82). So special attention needs to be paid to the peaks, and especially to endings; for example the exit from an office building should be as polished as the reception.

CHAPTER 7: EXPERIENCE DESTINATIONS

CASE STUDY 7.03

The Spine, Royal College of Physicians

LOCATION: LIVERPOOL, UK

ARCHITECT: AHR ARCHITECTS

BUILDING SERVICES ENGINEER: AECOM

COMPLETION: 2021

The Spine, the new northern home of the Royal College of Physicians in Liverpool, has been designed to achieve the highest standards of WELL assessment – including in air quality, filtration, biophilia, fresh air and materials. Completed In 2021, it won the British Council of Offices (BCO) Regional award for innovation in 2022. The concept and philosophy behind the design draw on the narrative of the human body and its abstract representation through architecture, biophilia and salutogenesis, factors that support health and well-being.

NASA's 'Clean Air Study' (1989) was used to help determine the most suitable plant species for air purification, which were then combined with highly specified air supply and filtration systems.[2] These significantly improve air quality to help increase people's health and cognitive performance by 10 to 20%.

Natural materials were used, including timber for ceilings, and carpets were made from recycled fishing nets to help to reduce fine dust particles in the atmosphere. The main entrance matting has bamboo infills to help clean people's shoes. Some floor areas are covered in a vinyl comprising 95% mineral products, which results in hardly any volatile organic compounds (VOCs) and off-gassing once laid. Specialist paint helps control toxic levels such as formaldehyde.

Furniture was one of the great challenges of the project, with only a few suppliers understanding the WELL standard and its requirement for low-VOC furniture, fixtures and equipment.

To comply with the WELL standard, the fresh air is supplied at 13 l/sec/person more than the 2019 BCO and current Building Regulations requirements, which reduces the CO_2 level to only 800 ppm, and should improve people's health and cognitive performance while they are in the building.

A Minimum Efficiency Reporting Value (MERV) 12 filtration rating system was used at The Spine. MERV values (developed by the American Society of Heating, Refrigeration and Air-Conditioning, ASHRAE) vary from 1 to 16; the higher the MERV value, the more efficient the filter is in trapping airborne particles. Another consideration is air flow through the HVAC system; leaving a dirty

◂◂ Figure 7.10: The Spine, Liverpool – the air-purifying entrance area

air filter in place or using a filter that is too restrictive may result in low air flow and possibly cause the system to malfunction. ASHRAE recommends MERV 6 or higher. LEED recommends a minimum of MERV 8. The college states that the MERV 12 system has the most positive impact in dealing with the smallest and most damaging of particulate matter (as particles below PM2.5 cannot be adequately filtered by the human body via the nostrils and so can make their way into the lungs; this has a significant detrimental health impact inside a building). MERV 12 filtration can remove up to 80% of these particles, fundamentally improving air quality.

Air-quality monitors are located every 300 square metres, with their data shared on PC monitors to ensure that people are aware of the air quality around them. Every PC has access to a dashboard with real-time environmental data relevant to the building and their own workspace. Sensors fitted into light fittings detect how spaces are used, how often and by how many.

Figure 7.11: A biophilic-inspired work area

Figure 7.12: A biophilic-inspired meeting room

Figure 7.13: The Spine's design encourages users to enjoy views over Liverpool.

A diverse group of people does not appreciate uniform temperatures, so workspaces have been designed instead to allow an optimal three-degree variance across the floor. Individuals can move to areas they feel most comfortable, and so, psychologically, they feel their personal needs are being catered for.[3]

It is the intention of the college team to measure longer-term health outcomes on visitors and members of staff in the new building. They will then be able to determine which features have an instant health impact.

Key points around air quality:

- Understand and measure the external air quality, consider noise and pollution.
- Agree the internal air quality brief, including fresh-air rates and quality, e.g. 14 l/sec/person, CO_2 under 800 ppm and high levels of filtration, F7.
- Consider natural ventilation; provide plenty of fresh air. Provide tall ceilings: 2.7 to 3 metres. Provide occupant control.
- Where ventilation systems are mechanical, consider underfloor/low-level supply and extract at a high level to avoid recirculation. Provide high-quality filtration.
- Select natural materials and furniture, fixtures and fittings to minimise VOCs; consider materials with a positive benefit on air quality, e.g. paint, natural materials, etc.
- Provide biophilic planting that improves air quality by absorbing VOCs.
- When the building is in use, provide openable windows, with sensors to inform when to open them. Use predictive analytics to understand when to open windows.
- As part of the FM plan, make sure all products used in the building are not harming the environment – for example soaps, detergents, paper and so on.
- Measure indoor air quality. Incorporate sensors that record air quality and raise alarms to provide real-time updates for users.
- Ensure a good cleaning regime, maintain ventilation systems, check and calibrate controls.
- Publish results and share best practice.

Figure 7.14: The use of natural materials, plentiful daylight, greenery and a central staircase promote well-being.

CREATING SCALED EXPERIENCES

Designing and creating an experience requires subtle handling. Like music, the combinations of notes, instruments, pace and volume must be carefully chosen. Similarly, whether workspace or retail, a range of environments cannot be served up with a single style. Even in an immersive experience, the environment itself is scattered with unique moments. Variety is what creates a dynamic experience.

Increasingly, work environments are providing wider choice for the user, from heavily extroverted interactions to quieter pathways for introverts. Providing a gradient of user journeys not only allows an experience to appeal to a wider variety of people, it holds the interest of those who have already visited by signalling that there is more to experience. The leisure and retail sectors are leading on this. As seen on a grand scale, the visitor experience for whisky brand Johnnie Walker in Edinburgh provides a feast for the senses (see case study 7.04), while for recent innovations in retail see Carrefour BlahBlah and Amazon Fresh (case study 7.05).

Figure 7.15: Johnnie Walker, Princes Street occupies the old House of Fraser department store on Edinburgh's Princes Street.

CASE STUDY 7.04:

Johnnie Walker, Princes Street

LOCATION: EDINBURGH, SCOTLAND, UK

DEVELOPER/ARCHITECTS/DESIGNERS: PARABOLA, EZ CONCEPT AND KEPPIE DESIGN

COMPLETION: 2020

Some buildings stand the test of time, their purpose reinvented while retaining cultural significance. Number 146 Princes Street is a landmark in the city of Edinburgh, originally built for banking then morphing from hotel to Scottish Liberal Club to various department stores from 1894, finally in 1953 becoming a House of Fraser department store. Whatever the building's purpose, it has always been a destination, a meeting place with remarkable views over Edinburgh Castle. However, as high-street shopping declined, House of Fraser closed, presenting an opportunity for Number 146 to reinvent itself once again.

The opportunity

In 2017 the property developer Parabola bought the site with an eye to reimagining it. Understanding its social capital and stature on the skyline, the firm sought to deliver a scheme celebrating its full potential and value.

Around this time drinks company Diageo wanted to find a building in Edinburgh to create a visitor experience for the bestselling Scotch whisky in the world, Johnnie Walker. The building was intended as a 'brand home' for visitors wishing to explore Johnnie Walker, its products and ultimately Diageo's distilleries across Scotland too. The project objective was to create the best whisky visitor experience in the world.

The experience

Parabola and Diageo focused on collaborating to deliver and shape a brand experience to engage all the senses. Each floor was given a specific purpose, such as sensory rooms and event space, fitted out in a variety of personalised finishes. During the process, both companies took the opportunity to enhance the historic building.

Figure 7.16: The Explorers' Bothy Bar offers a unique whisky-tasting experience.

The success of the project lies in the following:

- **A collaborative partnership of developer/landlord and tenant:** Both parties saw the potential of this building, which the strong brand vision from Diageo has brought to life.
- **The location:** It is a city-centre landmark destination, and iconic – echoing the history of the Johnnie Walker brand.
- **Immersive:** Johnnie Walker, Princes Street focuses on the senses to evoke the brand, including with sights, sounds, lighting and materials.
- **Materiality:** Extending the theme of whisky as a craft product, the history of the site, combined with a rich material palette steeped in craftsmanship, creates a destination where customers can live and breathe the brand. Materials have been chosen to reflect the origin and mood of the brand, e.g. tactile, high-quality materials such as oak cladding in the stairwell and copper-effect cladding on the walls of the bar.
- **Framed moments:** The view of Edinburgh castle from the rooftop bar is iconic, giving visitors an opportunity to pause, gaze out across one of the most famous cities in the world and take a photo. Johnnie Walker, Princes Street is crowned by two rooftop bars with a terrace overlooking the city's skyline and the castle.

Figure 7.17 (top): An immersive experience on the 'Journey of Flavour' tour

Figure 7.18: Visitors enjoy views of the city from the '1820 Rooftop Bar'

REWORKING THE WORKPLACE

CASE STUDY 7.05

Carrefour BlahBlah and Amazon Fresh

LOCATION: VARIOUS

COMPLETION: 2021

French supermarket brand Carrefour has introduced a 'slow' checkout till that allows customers and staff to talk and exchange news – hence its name, the 'BlahBlah' checkout.

This has been well received by customers and staff, creating positive social interactions for customers who may feel lonely and enabling Carrefour staff to feel recognised.[4] In an alternative system, Amazon Fresh stores introduced in the UK in 2021 offer a cashier-free experience that enables customers to walk straight out, for a quick and efficient shop. This is done through the use of overhead cameras and weight sensors on shelves, charging the customers directly to their Amazon account.

FRAMED MOMENTS

Is it possible to sum up the experience in a single image? In retail there is always an experiential moment which encapsulates the ethos of the brand. In the workplace, defined moments can be framed as vignettes. A row of seats positioned to look out at a specifically framed view while taking a break, or a project table located between two collaborating teams. These defined interventions are examples of moments of curated immersion and leave the user with a feeling of definition.

In a TikTok/Instagram world, perfect examples of framed moments within an experience destination are a 'selfie' or a curated four-second video posted to stories. In either case, the image or video is focused on capturing – for a moment – the experience of the place. These digital postcards act as a memento, and through social media, solidify the value of a place.

CASE STUDY 7.06

Selfie Factory and Tikky Town

LOCATION: LONDON, UK

COMPLETION: 2020

Selfie Factory is aimed at today's Instagram generation. It has a wide range of themed photobooth scenes based on backdrops found in popular Instagram posts. The set-ups create Instagram-ready pictures where the users simply need to strike a pose. Linked to Selfie Factory is Tikky Town, which is tailored for the TikTok audience, encouraging users to create their own content with more imaginative spaces. With changing rooms available, users can try different outfits and generate fun content for their social media.

Figure 7.19: The Selfie Factory in London – a playground for social media content creators

CHAPTER 7: EXPERIENCE DESTINATIONS

CASE STUDY 7.07

CapitaSpring

LOCATION: SINGAPORE

ARCHITECTS: BJARKE INGELS GROUP AND CARLO RATTI ASSOCIATI

DEVELOPER: CAPITALAND DEVELOPMENT

COMPLETION: 2021

CapitaSpring is Singapore's latest 51-storey integrated development, comprising a Grade A 'Office of the Future', a 299-unit serviced residence, retail, a four-storey public garden with social and activity spaces, a sky garden and a two-storey hawker centre.

The new 280-metre skyscraper integrates work, live and play spaces in a vertically connected environment. A 35 metre-high 'Green Oasis' is sandwiched between the office floors and residential units. Social and active spaces are spread out over four storeys of lush greenery and trees; the Green Oasis offers a reconnection with nature in the middle of the city and serves as usable social spaces that are open to the public. The rooftop skygarden is a 420-square-metre edible garden and urban farm, which will serve as a sustainable source of ingredients for a fine-dining restaurant by F&B-and-lifestyle group 1-Group on the same floor. In support of the government's drive towards a car-lite society and to promote healthy living, a cycle path, bike store and end-of-trip facilities are also included in the development.

CapitaSpring is a recipient of the Building and Construction Authority (BCA) Green Mark Platinum Award, one of the highest green building accolades in Singapore, and the BCA Universal Design Mark Gold^{PLUS} Award. The building construction achieved energy savings that exceed the BCA's base standard of 25%. The building includes water-efficient fittings, rainwater-harvesting systems and an energy-efficient central air-conditioning system, all of which support CapitaSpring's commitment to global sustainability.

Separately, to foster a sense of community within CapitaSpring, there is a Community Ambassador, who is pivotal to understanding the tenants' needs, curating social activities and also helping smaller companies to tap into the community network of other tenants within the building. This ecosystem is in place to boost employees' morale and well-being.

Cushman & Wakefield, Singapore relocated to CapitaSpring in May 2022. It was chosen because it offers a multifaceted workplace experience for the employees that supports the company's workplace ecosystem.

Figure 7.20: CapitaSpring's rooftop garden with views over Singapore

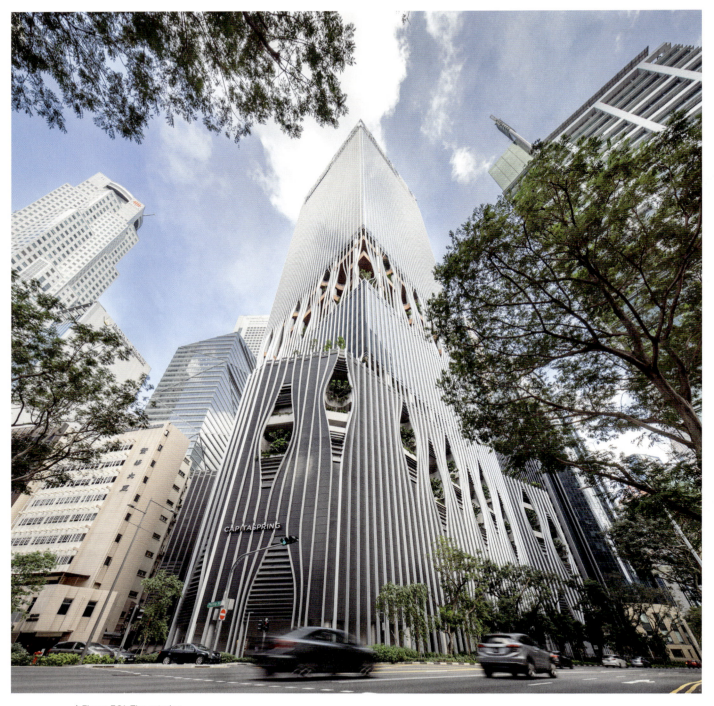

Figure 7.21: The exterior of CapitaSpring, Singapore

CHAPTER 7: EXPERIENCE DESTINATIONS

▲ Figure 7.22: CapitaSpring's Green Oasis lets users reconnect with nature.

> We created a destination office at CapitaSpring to reflect a post-pandemic new-age work culture. The new-age design promotes agility with multiple-use cases for the same space and individuality without compromising on collaboration and teamwork. All this, while supporting a hybrid way of working with total tech integration. We have successfully built an environment and a space that has enabled a strong return to office, client engagement through multiple events, and a superior experience for everyone who visits us or works here.

ANSHUL JAIN, CUSHMAN & WAKEFIELD'S MANAGING DIRECTOR, INDIA AND SOUTHEAST ASIA

CONCLUSION

Knowing how to handle and curate experience is a vital element in the designer's toolkit. Much has been learned from the hospitality, retail and leisure sectors that is now being deployed in the workplace. By purposefully and subtly manipulating all the senses, it is possible to create work environments that are varied, stimulating and social, and that support both collaboration and concentration.

LEARNING POINTS

Consider the following for successful experience destinations:

- a holistic understanding of the interconnections between people, purpose and place
- establishing a clear brand vision. Brand is the external view of an organisation, whereas culture is the internal perspective. Brand and culture need to reflect each other. Some workplace experiences are poor because they are all about brand and not about culture.
- promoting open connections to the wider urban landscape and community
- incorporating a variety of experiences at different scales of interaction for a number of user journeys
- framing moments that encapsulate the destination and ethos of the experience

PART III

PLACE

This is a pivotal moment in the story of work and the city. The impacts on the fabric and functioning of future cities will be significant. The scale could well be equivalent to the transformations of the late nineteenth century, with the introductions of passenger rail and underground train networks, new ways of building taller and the widespread introduction of electricity. They changed cities, and how their populations lived and worked, forever.

CHAPTER 8

Evolution of cities

INTRODUCTION

Fundamental change to our cities has happened only infrequently. In most instances this change has been triggered by the emergence of two factors. One is society's demand to alter aspects of city life that are not working well, and the other is the emergence of new technologies that provide the option to do things differently.

In the 2020s both of these factors are present and the mood for change is tangible. Many Western cities share the challenges of a lack of affordable housing, environmentally damaging practices and social inequalities. Calls for change to the status quo are being amplified by social media, activism and populist politics. Meanwhile, the internet is unlocking myriad new options for how we live our lives, how we shop and now how we work.

This is a pivotal moment in the story of the city. The impacts on the fabric and functioning of future cities will be significant. The scale could well be equivalent to the transformations of the late nineteenth century, with the introductions of passenger rail and underground train networks, new ways of building taller and the widespread introduction of electricity. These innovations all provided ways for cities to shift gears in ways that the majority of people welcomed. They changed cities forever, not just in the ways they were planned and built, but how they operated, and in how their populations lived and worked.

A SHORT HISTORY OF CITIES AND THE WORKPLACE

Cities have not always been synonymous with work. In early history, most people lived and worked in the small, decentralised rural communities that underpinned agricultural economies. The city, however, carried disproportionate power. It was where people brought their crops to trade; it was where the seats of government and military power were; and it was the birthplace of many inventions along with scientific and cultural developments.

With industrialisation came rapid evolution. Within a period of 50 years from 1800, buoyed by a new industrial workforce, the population of Manchester quadrupled from approximately 70,000 to 300,000.[1] Meanwhile, at the dawn of the nineteenth century, London became the epicentre of an increasingly efficient global trade network, and in the 1820s overtook Beijing as the largest city in the world.[2]

The only large organisations in ancient times were typically militaries; however, trade brought with it new commercial organisations, one of the earliest being the East India Company, founded in 1600.[3] These employed teams of staff to work on clerical activities – the beginnings of the modern service economy. And, in turn, these teams required purpose-built offices.

◂◂ Figure 8.01: Trade created the first economic purpose for cities.

▴ Figure 8.02: Industrialisation led to rapid urbanisation.

↑ Figure 8.03: The first large companies, such as the East India Company, gave rise to the first offices.

WORK AND THE OFFICE

The majority of discussions around the future of work assume that most people work in offices. It would be easy to forget that offices are only a recent invention (early 1700s), driven by the shift to a service-based economy that is yet to happen in many developing nations.

Even in the highly advanced economy of the UK, the reality is that most people don't work in offices. In fact most people don't work at all: 20% of people are too young to work, and 16% are too old;[4] 3% of people are seeking work at any given point and 13% choose not to work. In total that's just over half the UK population not working.[5]

Of those who do work, once you count cleaners, industrial operatives, shop assistants, teachers, doctors, lorry drivers, farmers, carpenters and a whole range of other occupations, the majority of working people do not work in offices. Furthermore, whether one would consider that fast-growing sectors such as life sciences will need office space in the future or something new is debatable.

So, offices are a recent invention. Most people don't work, and most of those who do don't work in an office. In the future we may need something which looks quite different to modern offices.

A TRIO OF INNOVATIONS

By the late nineteenth century, cities had become the dominant population centres in the UK. They generated new forms of industrial and service work and created real estate to house these activities in the form of factories and offices. The change measured against the previous century had been hugely significant, and there was even more to come as the result of three innovations that emerged between 1880 and 1900.

The seeds were sown earlier in the century, around the 1830s, with the Liverpool and Manchester Railway – the world's first inter-city railway.[6] The development and then consolidation of the UK's railway network was starting to affect the economies of distance. By the 1880s this had gathered pace, with the development of London's underground Circle Line (1884) and deep-level lines (1890).[7] Before this, most urban centres were what we would now call '15-minute cities', where people could walk from home to work. The passenger railway changed this. For the first time, people could live in a different location from their place of work.

Faced with the challenges of pollution, slums and crime in Victorian cities, a large section of the middle class elected to move out and escape to previously extra-urban locations.[8]

Meanwhile, in inner cities, an innovation of 1852, the safety elevator, together with new steel construction techniques, ushered in the development of tall commercial buildings (such as the 10-storey Home Insurance Building in Chicago of 1885) and changed urban topography. Large organisations could be accommodated in small footprints at greater densities and this refocused city centres as central business districts.

A third innovation went on to help define the twentieth century – electricity.

From the 1880s, in the space of a decade, cities became simultaneously and unrecognisably bigger, taller and brighter. During this period the relationship between work and the city was redefined, together with the spaces in

> ### METRO-LAND
>
> New public transport infrastructure is perhaps the most impactful form of value creation in our cities. It has unlocked most major development projects and changed the way that people live and move around our cities. One of the earliest and well-known examples of this is 'Metro-land' – a new swathe of suburbia facilitated by the development of London's Metropolitan railway.
>
> Over 100 years, London's population had increased from 1 million to 6 million.[9] The success of the city had not been matched by its infrastructure, and industrial uses in central areas combined with the coal hearth at home had created its infamous 'pea-soup' fog of sulphur dioxide. Many of those in London's burgeoning middle class dreamed of a better life in the country, a dream that would be facilitated by the development of the Metropolitan line.
>
> By the 1890s the line had been extended into the Middlesex countryside, connecting a series of small towns and villages to the capital. Combined with affordable mortgages and a promise of the fresh Chilterns air, Metro-land boomed. Between just 1921 and 1924 sales of train tickets rose 700%, and both commuting and suburbia were born.[10]
>
> The impact of suburbs on our cities was significant. Firstly, their footprint expanded dramatically. Secondly, a new typology of development, the detached or semi-detached suburban home, arrived, set in low-density plots with few other complementary uses. In London the legacy of Metro-land remains; aerial images reveal the north west corridor of grey development, a contrast to the less well-connected south east, which remains remarkably green.
>
> Once again major cities face a raft of social challenges. Will the internet and new modes of working unlock people's movements in the same way as the Metropolitan line once did? What lessons can be learned from this period about the form and location of the new housing needed to meet this demand?

which people work. At the dawn of the twentieth century, a new breed of office worker was carrying out corporate business in artificially lit towers at the heart of the fast-growing metropolis. A century later this vision continued to define how people worked.

For many, this period of innovation profoundly disconnected living from working, indelibly altering the form and purpose of our cities. Large daily commutes between separated working and living zones became typical, addressing some of the problems of pollution and cramped living, but also setting the stage for many of today's challenges.

CHANGE IN THE AIR

For most people living and working in Western cities, and particularly the poor, quality of life has been improving during the past century. More broadly, people have benefited from technologies such as cars, washing machines and new medical treatments. Lives are considerably more comfortable today than those of our great, great-grandparents.

However, since the millennium, it would be easy to see things differently. The global financial crisis of 2008 ushered in a period of economic stagnation, with challenging undercurrents for cities. A series of longer-range structural changes was developing. The UK, in common with many other Western economies, has experienced a chronic, systemic deficit of housing delivery relative to demand. Planning policy has promoted ever-denser cities, which has mainly taken the form of vertical increases in central areas. And around these urban issues lie a series of deeper societal challenges.

Progressive labour practices have resulted in a steady reduction in working hours during the past century. However, in recent years the trend has reversed for the professional classes. Those working in office-based jobs in major cities have been working longer (and in many cases excessive) hours, driven by corporate pressures and the availability of 'always-on' technologies.[11] When workers do get home, they are often distracted by these same technologies, which decreases the quality of family time.[12]

→ Figure 8.04: Life in dense urban centres is facing new challenges.

The associated reduction in free time for many has been amplified by increased commuting times. As the housing shortage has pinched, many people have been forced to accept longer, poorer-quality commutes in search of amenity and affordability.

At a macro level the perception of and call to action around inequalities of race, gender and wealth have reached a new high. In addition, unless climate action is taken swiftly, the scientific prognosis for the future of the planet is decidedly bleak. In combination, these push factors are causing people to leave big cities. Against the popular narrative of rapid global urbanisation (heavily skewed by the industrialisation of Asian and African nations) many large Western cities are de-urbanising, with populations shifting to smaller cities and extra-urban locations.[13]

Perhaps ironically, suburbanisation and densification, the century-old solutions to the ills of our cities, have created many of today's social challenges. The calls for change will once again be directed at cities, and technology is once again supplying fresh alternatives.

A NEW SOLUTION

The internet is fundamentally changing lives. What started as a reference and communication tool is now underpinning new economies, new ways of doing business and new ways of living our lives.

The internet is also causing seismic shifts in business: digital products, such as media subscriptions and software automations, cost a fraction of their physical equivalents. The consequence is that businesses are increasingly looking for ways to dispense with expensive labour and physical processes, and to move to digital equivalents. On the other hand, digital marketplaces and platforms are creating 'winner-takes-all' industries such as social-media platforms and online application stores. Network effects, which reward scale with more scale, act as a magnet for new customers, polarising demand and resulting in fewer, bigger market leaders. People want to be in places where they can interact with other people. This historically explains the success of the city centre, but now also explains the success of social media platforms. The physical world is increasingly having to compete with the digital world for people's attention.

The internet is even changing fundamental human concepts. Knowledge that was once scarce is now abundant and open. Communication that needed to be face-to-face is now instant and anywhere. Mass persuasion — which used to be the reserve of politicians and newspaper editors — can now be achieved by anyone with a Twitter account. And the evidence suggests that people are now more likely to trust machines than they are to trust other people.[14]

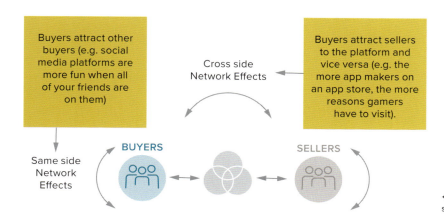

Figure 8.05: Network effects: scale is rewarded by more scale.

This has profound implications for society and for the future of cities. The most significant achievement of the internet has been to eliminate the penalties of distance. It is now possible to video call family members across the world instantly and without cost, to buy something without travelling to a shop, and now, of course, to work without visiting an office.

A MOMENT IN TIME

During the period of enforced distancing in the pandemic, people and businesses needed to find new ways of doing things. For many this was uncomfortable. However, over time, a significant number of people have benefited from these workarounds, and the duration of the pandemic enabled habits to be formed. Who would have considered attending a virtual doctor's appointment 10 years ago? Or taking part in a virtual spin class? Equally, who would have thought that the majority of clerical workers would shift to a new hybrid work model?

This once-in-a-century convergence of societal dissatisfaction and technological innovation creates a foundation for recent changes to become enduring. Particularly as the locus of work moves, broader city ecosystems will need to adapt to this change.

FOUR SCENARIOS FOR THE CITY OF 2040

When considering the long-term future, nothing can be certain. However, based on historic trends and the known impact of new technology, it is possible to predict some trends with greater certainty. For instance, it is now reasonably clear that significant climate action will be taken in response to global warming and that this will impact how buildings are designed and managed. It is also reasonably predictable that the population of the UK will continue to grow (albeit at a shallowing rate) and that this will give rise to the need for more housing. These kinds of factors can be baked into future predictions.

A second category of trends are those which are potentially high impact but carry low certainty. These can be described as 'critical uncertainties' and are used to form a scenarios grid when making future predictions. Following a piece of analysis and based on some of the trends considered above, there are two such critical uncertainties. First, the rate of urbanisation or de-urbanisation. Secondly the rate of adoption of new digital and virtual technologies. Plotted on a two-by-two matrix depicted in figure 8.06, these result in the following four scenarios.

HIGH VIRTUALISATION

4 SCENARIOS FOR THE FUTURE OF CITIES

▸ URBANISATION

LOW VIRTUALISATION

‹‹ Figure 8.06: Our analysis arrives at four scenarios for the city of 2040.

THE GRID

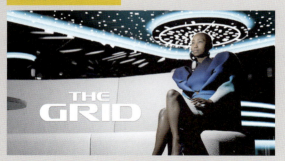

This is how most office workers lived during the pandemic: spending their days remote from the city centre but connecting with colleagues regularly through digital communication.

CROWDED CITIES are a thing of the past; high streets don't exist, replaced by huge distribution centres and drone delivery. People build strong communities virtually with less need for face-to-face interaction. The experience of exploring the virtual world is enough to create social connections, albeit people are never sure of the true identities of others. The physical workplace is much smaller, with the majority of work moved online.

PEOPLE LIVE AND WORK mostly online. Income is invested in online personas and virtual assets. Real estate is much more distributed than in the early 2000s. Location is less important, so over time languages, borders and nationalities fade, and the economy becomes truly global.

ENVIRONMENTALLY the energy required to maintain The Grid has been detrimental; albeit this is offset by less travelling and fewer buildings. Maintaining the virtual world is prioritised over the quality of the physical world with people living in small, functional and standardised units. The energy from urban heat islands is recycled back to the grid.

SOCIALLY interaction is virtual-first. Physical and mental health has deteriorated due to a lack of exercise, and fewer face-to-face interactions. The World Health Organization mandates time in physical health farms in natural environments to detox and build resilience for time online, and the majority of the world's developed nations are on preventative mood-stabilising medications.

GOVERNANCE is centralised over time as national borders and governments dissolve and a global government response is required to manage the increased energy demand. Global tech giants and international organisations set legislation and manage energy supply.

HERMITS

Distrustful and rejecting of modern society, people have chosen to live more de-centrally and shun the advances of the early 2000s.

CITIES have softened in economic and social significance. Global brands and organisations decline, as people want their patronage to benefit local communities. The loss to cities has translated to gains to smaller towns, the countryside, coast and mountains. Life has shifted from global to local, from excess to moderation with a strong focus on being environmentally and socially conscious – what's good for me needs to be good for us. Reliance on technology has been curbed, and society has fallen back on more traditional ways of working, centred on local relationships.

PEOPLE LIVE AND WORK in local communities; they make, grow and trade their own food and products, use local labour and materials, are self-sufficient and have a low carbon footprint. Global organisations are replaced by cottage industries. A return to nature is prioritised with more areas managed as national parks.

ENVIRONMENTALLY the use of renewable energy in local communities dominates. Global carbon emissions fall as communities are smaller and more self-sufficient. Buildings are designed and constructed using local skills, materials and labour.

SOCIALLY people are strongly connected to local language and culture. Communities look after themselves and become more insular and tribal. Deglobalisation leads to a loss of international awareness and knowledge-exchange, sending growth negative.

GOVERNANCE is decentralised across communities, which drives efficiency and democracy at a local level. Wariness of others and xenophobia experience a resurgence.

CHAPTER 8: EVOLUTION OF CITIES

HYPER-REALITY

Here is the future envisaged by many science-fiction movies: a dense urban environment, where augmented and virtual technologies are overlaid on the physical fabric and form an important part of how we live our lives.

DENSE CITIES have become engines for virtually augmented experiences. From shopping to working and entertainment, sustainable energy sources and cheap tech offset the negative repercussions of density by allowing for immersive virtual activity. People are comfortable in both the physical and virtual worlds, which are starting to blur. Experience and human connection are elevated by bringing the two together. Augmentation achieved through contact lenses pervades day-to-day activities such as work and leisure.

PEOPLE LIVE in dense cities for proximity benefits but achieve space and amenity through entering virtual worlds. The workplace has high quality-physical hubs in key locations, connected through digital twins and the metaverse to maintain a consistent workplace experience regardless of location or real estate costs. Physical and virtual environments evolve in parallel and are often interchangeable.

ENVIRONMENTALLY renewable energy dominates, and regional heating systems manage distribution and consumption. The interconnection of physical and virtual environments requires constant reconfiguration, which has driven a circular economy approach to construction and supply chains.

SOCIALLY wearables and technology implants are common, aimed at facilitating human performance and measurement, enabling people to shift seamlessly from the virtual to real worlds. As new technology emerges, a social divide grows between those who can afford it and those who cannot.

GOVERNANCE is centralised over time and national governments work together to manage climate change. Large tech conglomerates grow in influence, and now rival national governments for economic and social impact. Corporation and robot tax is increased to support infrastructure and renewable energy.

SOCIAL ANIMALS

This group largely represents the society in which humans have lived since the industrial era. It is typified by high-density, face-to-face contact.

CITIES are dense, large and diverse, putting strains on resources and infrastructure. The biggest cities have exploded in size, creating greater contrast with smaller towns. Neighbourhoods have expanded vertically and housing blocks have become mini villages. Technology has moved on but takes a back seat to face-to-face interactions. Consumerism prevails, but costs have risen, including housing costs. The commute to work is packed and inconvenient.

PEOPLE LIVE AND WORK in high-density environments. Personal space is a luxury. Commerce is king, and branded experiences lead leisure. Organisations mirror this when it comes to building culture and employee loyalty. Parks and green space are heavily trafficked and managed with strict time allowances for visitors.

ENVIRONMENTALLY many of today's issues remain or have worsened; climate change remains a looming threat. Climate migration has been directed at major centres, exacerbating infrastructure failings. New food production methods such as urban farming have taken off as supply chains have started to dry up.

SOCIALLY people become more segregated across communities of haves and have-nots. Slums grow in mega cities and a new global elite emerges. Presence privilege is pervasive.

GOVERNANCE and power are increasingly devolved to powerful city mayors, who control infrastructure-spend and manage public resources. Cities work together to manage migration and levy corporation tax to support population growth.

It is important to note that these scenarios present polarising bookends for our cities of the future. Most probably the future will be a mix of all these scenarios. Inertia dictates that the most popular scenario will be the one most closely resembling the status quo (i.e. Social Animals). However, looking back to other major periods of change, we could be surprised by rapid development particularly of The Grid and perhaps Hyper Reality. Those with young families and long commutes (an important element of the workforce) might gravitate towards The Grid, whereas younger people seeking excitement might be drawn towards Hyper Reality.

The likely unifying result of scenarios such as these will be an increasing variety of ways in which people choose to live and work in the future. Nine-to-five, five days per week in an office will no longer be an axiom for how we work. Some people may choose to live at much greater distances from their place of work. Some may even choose to live or indeed be told that their job is being relocated abroad. The design of cities and workplaces will therefore need to adapt to increasingly heterogeneous workforces and modes of working.

BACK TO THE FUTURE

Movies provide an interesting lens through which to view contemporary preoccupations about our cities and how they might evolve. Fritz Lang's iconic *Metropolis* presents a highly stylised futuristic city, where the dark underbelly of workers is crowned by a beautiful Utopia. Inspired by the development of New York in the 1920s, the film speaks to contemporary concerns about social inequalities in the increasingly inhumane, vast metropolises that were starting to emerge. Much later, Katsuhiro Otomo's cyberpunk cult hit *Akira*, addressed concerns around pollution and crime in 1980s Japan.

Common to most visions of the future is an increasingly dense, tall and brutalist urban form (*Dredd/Fifth Element*) in which automation and technological integration are central (*Blade Runner/AI/Minority Report*) and resource pressures prevail (*Interstellar/Avatar/Hunger Games*). Many films envisage a form of apocalyptic event which has defined the city, be it rising sea levels (*Cloud Atlas*), a nuclear disaster (*Akira/Logan's Run/Mad Max*), war (*The Day After*) or pandemic (*I Am Legend/12 Monkeys*).

Does it just help to sell cinema tickets to predict gloomy futures or is there more in it than that? In general, life in cities has been getting better, but many still look back through rose-tinted spectacles to a simpler pastoral life in low-density neighbourhoods.

As we contemplate the future of cities, it's important to be mindful that popular narratives such as those shown in movies can in fact drive us towards delivering the future they envisage (see Robert Shiller's work on 'Narrative Economics').[15] This underlines the need for city designers to disassociate ingrained mindsets of what cities might or should be and start with a blank page based on their own assessment of the facts.

« Figure 8.07: Visions of the future skew towards dense dystopic outcomes.

TEN STEPS TO A SUCCESSFUL NEW NORMAL

Dealing with uncertainty will become a key skill for those creating and managing successful places. Cities that respond to the needs of their inhabitants are economically and socially desirable; however, the needs of the individual and the needs of society have, to a degree, been put in conflict through these changes. Workers who have dispensed with their commute can save money, spend more time with their family and invest more in their local communities. However, this comes at the expense of their colleagues who benefited from regular face-to-face tuition, and the owner of the city-centre coffee shop that they used to visit. Can these positions be married? The following section contains 10 proposals to reinvigorate our cities.

1 Lower the cost of public transportation

If city centres, and therefore society, benefit from the presence of high-value workers who are now minded to use them less, one solution would be to displace some or all of the cost of public transport back onto the taxpayer. Heavily subsidised or even free public transport has been adopted in many cities across the world, including the entire country of Luxembourg (where public transport is free).

2 Reinvent the nine-to-five

By creating a flexible workday, it would be possible to alleviate congestion on roads and trains. Alternative ways of delivering work hours, such as four-day weeks and compressed hours, also provide new opportunities.

3 Improve rolling stock

By encouraging more people on to public transport and improving the experience (tables/wi-fi), the commute could be a productive time. This being the case, the time spent in the office could be contracted, to say 10–4, without any loss of productivity.

4 Make cities fun

Coming into the city centre should mean high-octane, immersive and interactive experiences that cannot be achieved at home, and businesses will need to find new ways to commercialise or capture the value of this engaged footfall.

5 Combine experiences

Advantage can be found in co-location between workplaces, retail and leisure, at a centre and at an asset level. New hybrid round-the-clock products will emerge that are not neatly defined by previous real estate definitions.

6 Build new homes in new locations

If people commute less frequently, they will often be willing to accept longer commutes on the days that they do so. This will start to alleviate the pressure on some big cities and provide opportunities to build economically sustainable homes in areas of existing low-cost land with high amenities.

7 Level up

As virtual connections grow in importance, the ecosystems of physically distant cities will start to join up. There are fewer challenges to delivering infrastructure in smaller, less dense cities, which provides an opportunity to promote and invest in these cities as a means for delivering growth.

8 Regreening

As more cities shift to lower reliance on cars, there is an opportunity to pedestrianise and deliver greening initiatives such as those in Copenhagen – all-electric buses, low-cost bike rental and generous parks.[16] Greening cities provides health benefits and a better experience for those living or visiting them. Strength of placemaking will become a defining competitive factor. Outdoor spaces even present opportunities for distributed work and meeting places, such as those proposed in the Parisian plans to turn the Champs-Élysées into 'an extraordinary garden'.[17]

⑨ Address corporate culture

Fun has been shown to deliver significant commercial benefits such as team cohesion, reduced churn and talent attraction. The option to divide work typologies between the home and the office provides an opportunity to make office-based work exciting, interactive and fun.

⑩ Build 15-minute cities[18]

An alternative method of reducing the penalties of distance is to bring all amenities in small order to everyone's doorstep and distribute these across a broader city ecosystem. This might be possible in urban-edge locations where the density of residents supports the economic case for commercial operations.

These proposals address the ambitions to (a) reduce inconvenience to workers and residents such that a more level playing field is created with working from home, and (b) increase the pull factor of city centres in a way that creates a new value proposition to reward the inconvenience of the commute. It is through these mechanisms that cities will retain vibrancy and purpose.

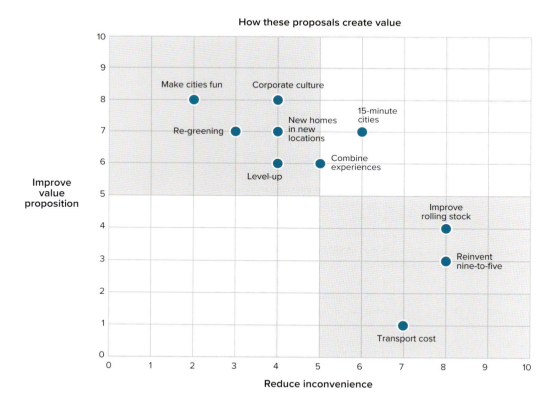

Figure 8.08: Value can be created through removing inconvenience and adding reward.

CONCLUSION

The shift being experienced in the 2020s is so significant it has raised many fears, ranging from concerns that workforces will dissolve through lack of social contact to an office-market collapse, leaving city centres as bleak ghost towns.

We should take comfort that cities have been through major changes on this scale before and have emerged more successful as a consequence. Rather than holding back the tide of change, there is an opportunity to embrace the new normal in a way that addresses the manifest challenges that people of the early twenty-first century face. Change brings the opportunity to take back free time, to mitigate climate issues, to live more human-centric lives, and make city centres exciting and fun. It also provides the opportunity to reposition office work, not as a chore to be endured, but rather a purpose-giving element of the week.

As with any period of change, it is the navigation of the transformation that is the biggest challenge, rather than the choice of destination. The challenge for urban designers and those who work in the real estate sector will be to actively manage the transition to the new normal in a way that acknowledges uncertainty, creates flexibility, addresses financial risks, manages obsolescence and proposes bold new solutions to yesterday's problems.

LEARNING POINTS

- The spark for change to the urban form comes when society demands change and new technologies are available to deliver alternatives. We have seen this in the early twentieth century, when the railway enabled people to escape urban ills to better lives in new suburbs.
- The 1880s provides an example of significant urban change as passenger rail, steel construction, the safety elevator and electrification all came about at a similar time. Within a short space of time, our cities grew outwards, upwards and brighter.
- In the 2020s change is being demanded in response to housing affordability, environmental sustainability, social inequalities and lack of free time. The way we design cities and real estate has been a significant contributor to these issues, and the real estate sector should expect to find itself under the spotlight to change.
- The internet is radically changing the nature of working, shopping and living. It is breaking fundamental constructs such as knowledge, communications, influence and trust, and it is changing the nature of business through scale economies and network effects. At a city level, the internet threatens to break the penalties of distance upon which urban economics are predicated.
- De-urbanisation and virtualisation will change the make-up of our future cities. The need for everything to be done in person in dense urban environments is softening, which opens the door to new ways of living and working. Our cities are likely to become more distributed.
- Solutions can be found through eliminating the inconveniences of commuting and through providing a new value proposition to come into city centres. Human-centric models will emerge which reduce the pain of travelling and in which the city centre doubles down as a place for excitement and interaction.

CHAPTER 9

The physical-virtual interface

INTRODUCTION

Ever since the use of the first stone tools, humans have augmented their capabilities using technology. By leveraging technological processes humans have been able to become more productive — a simple fact which explains most of the history of human advancement.

Early automations such as water- and wind-powered wheels enabled work tasks to be delivered with reduced human effort. This took a big leap forward in the Industrial Revolution, when steam power created huge production efficiencies. In doing so, it broke a millennia-old model for how people worked, changing the economic structure of the UK and creating new property typologies at the heart of powerful industrialised cities.

Moving through the twentieth century, this symbiosis of man and machine became the normal way of working.[1] Linear work processes on production lines created new roles, where, arguably, humans themselves became another cog in the machine rather than being responsible for cranking the handle.[2]

And now significant technological advancement is once again reshaping the relationship between humans and technology in a way that will profoundly impact the nature of work and redefine what we mean by a workplace.

DIGITAL WORK

The late twentieth century brought with it two of the most significant inventions in history: the computer and the internet. Modern clerical work is unimaginable without them, and hence workplaces have largely been crafted around their interface.

Building on early logic-based calculators such as the abacus or the Babbage Difference Engine, and employing new electronic foundations, the first computers were created.[3] However, the early machines were very different from those of today, more a feature of the old industrial economy than the worker-oriented service economy that the world was moving towards.

At this point, humans and machines still didn't talk to each other well. Interfaces took the form of binary switches and outputs, and while this might have been acceptable in a lab, computers in the clerical workplace required more ergonomic solutions. Consequently, the output of these logic-based calculations started to be visualised using lit pixels on digital displays, with users influencing the form of these pixels using peripheral input devices such as switches and keyboards. These were the first physical-virtual interfaces.

⇠ Figure 9.01: Richard Arkwright's Cromford Mills, Derbyshire, was the birthplace of the modern factory system.

CHAPTER 9: THE PHYSICAL-VIRTUAL INTERFACE

Figure 9.02: The first computers were functional but lacked an ergonomic interface for the user.

Humans, however, still felt more comfortable interacting with other humans. In response, some early robotics deployed forms of anthropomorphic design to humanise the robots and make the experience more natural.[4] From this point on, the stage was set for higher-fidelity visualisations that more closely approximated non-virtual interactions. This was delivered through a mix of better visualisation hardware, a radical increase in processor speed and a new wealth of creative talent focusing on these digital interfaces.[5]

At the same time, communications technology was expanding rapidly. During the latter half of the twentieth century the incentive for speed in the services sector significantly accelerated innovation. The fixed-line telephone had taken almost a century to achieve 95% adoption; the cell phone achieved the same feat in less than 20 years.[6] For document transfer, the fax replaced the post for urgent communications. Subsequently, emails replaced both for most forms of communication.

Those using an email account and occasionally browsing the web in the 1990s could hardly have imagined that they were standing on the tip of a gargantuan iceberg that would have transformed how we work just 30 years later. Cloud computing, the mobile internet, big data, artificial intelligence and machine learning have fundamentally changed how we live, work and shop in the 2020s.

The integration of humans and machines has become inextricable and is heading deeper. However, has the interface between the two changed significantly?

PHYSICAL-DIGITAL INTERFACES IN THE TWENTY-FIRST-CENTURY WORKPLACE

Most modern offices are designed to support the interface between humans and computers. Buildings have been redesigned over the past 50 years to accommodate new requirements for service media and cabling, rendering obsolete some older stock not capable of doing so. For some operations, the speed of communications is a significant consideration in building selection, and connectivity benchmarks such as the digital certification system WiredScore play an increasing role in decision-making.[7]

More obviously, most businesses fit out their offices on the assumption that for the majority of the day employees will need to be sitting in front of a monitor. Although the percentage of allocated desk space within office layouts has been steadily decreasing and agile touchdown spaces for laptops are more common, rows of monitors still define the mechanical look and feel of most corporate offices.[8]

As businesses have gone digital, the shift has been away from interacting with paper and towards interacting with data. Remote and intangible cloud-based file storage has replaced rows of filing cabinets, and greater aptitude in keyboard use and voice recognition has replaced many typing pools. The modern office now also better understands and adapts to its occupiers. Internet-connected sensors enable improved energy management, localised environmental settings that respond to user preferences, and measurement of utilisation to better predict when space will be required. The integration between the human occupiers of space and the supporting digital technologies is evolving. However, the primary physical-virtual interface of monitors, which locks workers to rows of desks, remains a barrier to workplace reinvention.

The use of monitors has in fact become more important in recent years. For office workers, the shift from paper files to screens has been progressive. However, until recently most meetings were conducted away from screens, either in-person or on conference phones. While video calling existed,[9] the shift to video meetings[10] in the workplace was sharply precipitated by the pandemic and has not reverted as working patterns have moderated.[11] Hybrid meetings, where some participants dial in, have become the default, and this has led to an increased need for physical screens in the workplace.

Compared to face-to-face meetings, a shift to video calling may seem like a step backwards. But old-style meetings using just an audio line did not enable attendees to experience visual nuance and body language. For many who work as part of global teams or with international clients, the video meeting experience has been liberating. For some, this modal shift has allowed them to see their clients and colleagues for the first time. For others who might have been invisible or subordinated in face-to-face meetings, the non-hierarchical format of video calls has rebalanced power in their favour.

SMART BUILDINGS

In response to the Covid-19 pandemic and the rapid emergence of this new work format, there has also been an acceleration in the ways that buildings themselves form part of the physical-virtual interface. The immediate pandemic response was focused on health concerns and, assisted by digital technologies, the operation of workplaces reoriented around this. Features included:

Figure 9.03: The pandemic significantly accelerated the adoption of video calling in the workplace – data aggregated from Microsoft Announcements, 2020.

- **Scanning for infection:** Operated in airports and restaurants for some time, temperature-scanning devices have been deployed in office reception areas as a means of screening for infected individuals.
- **Contactless design:** Infrared-enabled, touch-free taps; app-controlled coffee-machines; powered doors; touch-free toilets; voice-powered operations; and pre-programmed elevators are all on the rise.
- **Capacity management:** In many offices, desk booking was instigated for the first time to ensure that new capacity constraints addressed social-distancing rules.

The health benefits of contactless surfaces and the capacity-management and planning benefits of desk booking are likely to endure. A key benefit of digitally controlled interfaces is that they provide a wealth of data on usage and resource allocation that can be used to more effectively manage offices in the future. Based on this principle, the following elements will play a more significant role:

- **Virtual receptionist:** Fully autonomous or remotely serviced digital receptions offer a low-cost entry solution. Visitors are requested to submit their contact details directly into a cloud-based database. Digital receptions can be integrated with resource allocation such as meeting-room bookings or used to improve the customer journey (e.g. through repeat knowledge of the visitor's favourite coffee).
- **Predictive resource allocation:** Artificial intelligence (AI) can be used to spot patterns in resource consumption (e.g. fixed-desk settings, printer usage, energy usage and need for air recirculation). AI can then adjust building supplies, power down systems and conserve energy.
- **Predictive diary management:** AI can act as a personal assistant to identify the best time for a face-to-face meeting, based on the typical usage pattern of meeting attendees.[12] This will be a key tool in managing the complexities of hybrid working.
- **Meeting-room technologies:** To create a level playing field for virtual and in-person meeting attendees, conferencing webcams with smart zooming technology are becoming the norm. The camera picks up the active speaker and focuses the video feed on that person rather than the broader meeting room.

THE NEXT LEAP – VIRTUAL WORLDS AND THE METAVERSE

Video calling still lacks the immersion needed to tempt most of us away from higher-quality, real-world interactions. Hence there is a prize for achieving greater fidelity. In the early 2020s this started to appear as 3D virtual environments began creating a richer and more ergonomic experience.

A number of closed virtual environments have been designed which allow dispersed workplace teams to better simulate face-to-face environments.[13,14] These typically allow a team member in the form of an avatar to navigate a virtual space and interact with other users. Some of these environments have been designed to simulate a real-world space, for instance by using the same floor plate as the team's physical office or by using photo-realistic avatars. While this technology is still in its infancy, we should expect rapid improvements in virtual-physical fidelity, and with this a breaking down of the barriers to adoption.

CASE STUDY 9.01

Google Starline

LOCATION: GOOGLE OFFICES, USA

Helping to solve the universal problem of co-workers, family and friends wanting to be physically together when it is not possible, Google is developing Project Starline. An immersive form of remote communication, it is based on videoconferencing to allow a more natural conversation to take place between two people. Through its 'research in computer vision, machine learning, spatial audio and real-time compression', Google's vision for the future of videoconferencing comprises a video booth in which users can interact with fully three-dimensional and life-size images of each other in real time.[15] The intended effect is to enable users to feel that the other person is sitting right across from them.

This screen-based system is intentional in providing an alternative to headset-based conferencing systems, for example virtual-reality headsets, which have not proved their worth to consumers in user-experience studies due to their weight and lack of comfort.

This digital style of communication, known as telepresence, was first deployed in industry by Cisco back in 2006, with their CEO citing Star Trek's 'holodecks' as the inspiration for the venture. In Google's own terms, telepresence can be defined as 'recreating the appearance and sound of a remote user with sufficient quality to enable all conversational cues, while retaining the simplicity of just sitting down and talking with a person in real life'.[16]

Google worked on the project for a few years before announcing it in May 2021. Since then, it has conducted some promising early-stage user trials which have found improvements in important communication signals which are often lacking in 2D forms of communication. These include increased non-verbal behaviours, such as head nods and hand gestures, memory recall and attentiveness to the other user.

Currently, Project Starline is only available in a few Google offices in the US, but after the technology is fully developed and tested the next goal is to make the system more accessible and affordable for business users.

Figure 9.04: As if you are there: physical-virtual meetings via Google's Starline

Perhaps more than the visual experience, however, these virtual worlds unlock serendipity (one of the drivers of the value of place identified in chapter 6). Video meetings have been criticised for being too formulaic and structured; they lack the ability to tap someone on the shoulder or bump into someone by chance. Virtual environments on the other hand specifically cater for both of these and therefore offer an important step in unlocking the digital interface.

Moving forward, the binary choice of holding a meeting in the physical or the virtual world is likely to blur further. The use of augmented reality will start to create digital overlays on the physical world which 'bring to life' virtual attendees. Meanwhile, for those attending remotely, virtual reality will simulate the experience of being in the room with their physical counterparts. The future workplace will be a seamless blend of the physical and the virtual.

A separate but related innovation comes in the development of metaverses – immersive virtual worlds. The fundamental differences between a metaverse and a closed virtual environment are that (1) the metaverse is open to the public; (2) parcels in the metaverse can be bought and sold; and (3) the metaverse offers the opportunity for commercial activities based on blockchain technologies and Web3 (also known as Web 3.0; a new iteration of the World Wide Web) principles. Metaverses, which are therefore loftier in ambition than closed environments, are less likely to be applicable to the workplace than virtual environments in the medium term. The interaction and serendipity benefits sought by workplace teams can be delivered without the cost and requirements for openness of metaverses. In the longer term, however, the potential to create whole new worlds based on transparent commercial rules and logic, but without some of the inconveniences of the real world, offers tantalising opportunities to define the nature of reality.

	VIRTUAL ENVIRONMENT	METAVERSE
Example	Gather/Teamflow	Decentraland/The Sandbox
Public access	Closed/Private	Open/Public
Underlying technology	Local/Cloud-based code	Blockchain
Economic foundations	No economy	Crypto/NFTs
Governance	Centralised	Decentralised
Costs	Fee/Subscription/Free	Free to use/Ownership costs
Current applications	Meetings/Calls/Workspace	Advertising/Trade/Entertainment

↑ Table 9.01: Often confused, virtual worlds and metaverses have fundamentally different foundations and applications.

SMART PEOPLE

The true convergence of human and machine has long been envisaged in science fiction in the form of the cyborg – a physically augmented human. Is this still science fiction?

It could be argued that all humans are now augmented. It is rare today for most people to be more than a couple of metres away from their smartphone. These 'phones' are now in fact supercomputers by the standards of the Atanasoff-Berry machine.[17] Importantly, they also benefit from high-speed internet access. Hence modern humans can augment their own intelligence and knowledge anytime, anywhere, at the click of a button (or the swipe of a finger), and they do so with great regularity. The average person accesses the internet from their phone 300 times per day.[18] These are the primary physical-virtual interfaces of the early twenty-first century, and, unlike monitors, they are untethered.

They now allow people to access work and communicate with others anywhere. Notifications and reminders make their presence continuous, to the effect that the work has become a 24/7 'always-on' phenomenon.[19] Perhaps more than anything else in modern history, the smartphone and mobile internet have reshaped how we live and have recast our relationship with the workplace.

This is, however, only the start of the story. A smartphone still involves a screen and a small one at that, which is a poor approximation of real-world interactions. More immersive technologies, such as Oculus Rift headsets and Google Glass, offer a glimpse at what is to come. Both are prescient but lacking adoption, mainly due to form issues. Wearing a large headset or a visible camera can create barriers to interaction rather than resolving them. The solutions lie in making the form of the devices less intrusive, and this innovation is already under way. Mojo

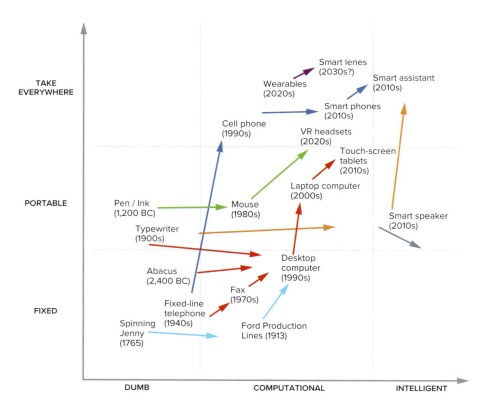

Figure 9.05: Over time, physical-virtual interfaces have become smarter and more portable.

Lens, for instance, provides a true heads-up display in the form of an invisible contact lens.[20] This allows the user to augment physical reality with information from the internet, which could for instance include the notes for your presentation or an alert that it is the birthday of the person you are speaking with. Being an exam invigilator will be a very difficult, and perhaps unnecessary, role in the future, if people can cheat at will and no one needs to remember anything.

Looking forward, the evolution of the physical-virtual interface will become more integrated and more immersive. Stockholm-based co-working space Epicenter has implanted workers with rice-sized processor chips that allow for touchless security and printer queue access.[21] Elsewhere Elon Musk has launched a programme which aims to create brain-computer interfaces using neural implants that enable the user to control external devices by thinking about them.[22]

For the possibilities of greater immersion, just look to the military and to theme parks, both of which are able to spend disproportionately on immersive experience and whose technology will inevitably trickle down to consumer markets. Virtual-reality applications in both areas have come a long way from the early explorations of the 1990s. Graphics are now fully faithful to real-world environments, with rich and complex worlds limited only by the creativity of the designer. Meanwhile, the overwhelming focus on the senses of sight and sound is now diversifying into olfactory and haptic immersion through the use of suits and diffusers.

Beyond reinventing the workplace, these technologies offer the prospect of changing the world, or perhaps creating a new one.

CASE STUDY 9.02

Madison Square Garden Sphere

LOCATION: LAS VEGAS, USA

COMPLETION: 2023

While it might be assumed that virtualisation will soften the need for real estate venues, in the early 2020s the best virtual and augmented experiences still require significant physical hardware to operate. The cost and sometimes size of this hardware mitigates against home or distributed use and creates an opportunity for new physical-virtual experience centres.

One such is the Madison Square Garden (MSG) Sphere in Las Vegas. Costing a reported $1.8 billion, the 100 metre tall, spherical venue will include wraparound LED screens covering 15,000 square metres, together with 160,000 speakers.[23] It is described as a 'whole new medium and multisensory platform'.[24]

The sound rig uses beam-forming technologies to create uniform audio across the venue.[25] MSG's audio partner Holoplot has used the same technology to create unique audio experiences for multiple listeners in one room.[26] For example, different people in the same space could hear the audio output from a movie in different languages. Meanwhile, the fully programmable LED display will be the largest in the world with a resolution over 100 times higher than HD TV, creating very high real-world fidelity.[27]

Using cameras and projection technology invented specifically for this concept, the exterior of the dome can be made to virtually disappear by superimposing real-time images of its surroundings onto the sphere.[28]

Initially the use of the MSG Sphere will concentrate on live concerts and eSports. However, it is also expected to act as a conference venue and a home for corporate events and product launches.

TECHNOLOGY	WHAT IS IT?	CURRENT EXAMPLES	FUTURE WORKPLACE OPPORTUNITIES
Smart sensors	Internet-connected sensors which ingest data from the physical environment	Modern IoT sensors now employ 5G and Edge computing to reduce latency and increase power	Thermal / sensory customisation, energy efficiency, environmental adaptions / predictive design
Smart appliances	Appliances in the home / workplace which adapt to sensor input or in response to predefined rules	Samsung washing machines which adjust water based on weight and dirtiness of clothing	Energy reduction, environmental automation, Automated supplies reordering
Visual Immersion	Eyewear that immerses vision with digitally created inputs	Varjo-headset enables high-fidelity vision with variable focus and peripheral res	Improved experience in virtual / hybrid meetings. Diminishing barriers to distance
Haptic Immersion	Bodywear that simulates sense of touch to simulate physical interactions	HoloSuit prototype includes 9 haptic feedback devices covering all limbs	Improved experience in virtual / hybrid meetings. Ability for tactile interaction with people / objects
Intelligent HUDs	Screens / eyewear that allows user to display additional data connected to what they see	Mojo Vision's contact lens identifies road directions, calendar appointments etc	Productivity gains by serving up information / data to worker connected with their current subject matter
Augmented reality	Digital technologies that superimpose virtual objects onto real world environments	IKEA app allows user to test out how products will look in consumers' homes	Improvement of remote meetings through digital replication of remote attendee / object
Wearables	Sensors and smart technologies that the user wears, and often collect data on physical interactions	Apple Watch, Fitbit, used to measure heart rate, exercise and oxygen levels	Medical monitoring / clothing that adjust to environmental conditions
Subcutaneous Implants	Processor chips inserted under the skin of the user that monitor their body or credentialise the wearer	Epicenter (Stockholm) implants workers with chips	Security access. Medical monitoring used to pre-empt medical issues
Neural Implants	Neural chip or brain-computer interface (BCI) that connects the brain to external digital equipment	Battelle has deployed a BCI which allowed a disabled man to feel his hand	Memory and concentration gains. Amelioration of degenerative conditions
Smart Assistants	Intelligent devices that can interact with the user / pre-empt requirements to deliver administrative services	Alexa, Siri etc allow user to get smart prompts and responses via the internet	Automation of administrative / reception tasks and roles. Smart scheduling
Artificial Intelligence	A machine-based intelligence that can perceive its environment, learn and in cases act autonomously	LegalRobot reviews and critiques legal documents	Automation of higher-order clerical work, enabling corporates to achieve greater operational leverage
Digital Twins	A digital model intended to faithfully replicate a physical equivalent	Singapore has built a city twin to help with traffic flow and development	Simulations. City and transport planning
Metaverses	A new visual form of the internet in which users can interact in an open virtual reality space	Sandbox / Decentral and allow users to buy plot and trade using crypto	The carrying out of many work tasks in virtual spaces with separate economic conditions

Table 9.02: Existing cutting-edge technology will unlock new ways of working in the future.

WHAT DOES THIS MEAN FOR WORK AND OFFICES?

For most of modern history, work has been on a journey of centralisation and agglomeration, as companies found benefits in bringing more and more people into the same physical space. In today's society this has taken the form of central offices, built to accommodate large numbers of service workers. Technology however is breaking down the need for and benefits of this physical centralisation.

Looking forward, some work tasks are likely to be entirely relocated to virtual environments. This will be industry and task dependent, and to some extent related to the desired culture of the corporation. Those industries that are already comfortable using digital technologies and those with globally oriented teams are more likely to use the advances in virtualisation to access a broader talent pool. Meanwhile others that have a local market interface or a reliance on high-quality collaboration will rely less on virtual delivery.

However, even for those workplaces that are physically oriented, it is becoming clear that a high percentage of all interactions in the future will be augmented in some way by virtual technologies. This is not a surprising outcome; it is a natural evolution of a journey starting with water mills and fixed-line telephones. It is the spurt of adoption of virtual technologies seen in the pandemic that was not predicted, nor was it generally anticipated how well most people would adapt to new modes of communication. Now the role of workplace managers and workplace designers has been significantly complicated by a need to interpret how the model will settle down, even as the technology is still evolving.

Looking forward, a critical question for the workplace is the extent of reliance on monitors and fixed-desk settings. On the one hand, video calling has re-emphasised the need for dedicated video interfaces. On the other, new untethered screens, headsets and even contact lenses offer potential for more agile ways of working in the future.

Table 9.03: Changing nature of human relationship with digital environment

PRE-PANDEMIC	PANDEMIC	NEAR FUTURE
SEPARATE AND OBSERVING	CONNECTED BUT SEMI-IMMERSED	FULLY IMMERSED
Conference Calls	**Microsoft Teams + VC**	**VR + Metaverse**
Connection was a choice.	Immediate connection and availability is assumed.	'always on' working takes on employees.
Focused on talking about what is going to be done and doing it later.	Real time, cloud-hosted documents, teams are actively working together while on calls.	Will evolve to enable more personal control.
	Work happens 24/7.	More agnostic and autonomous working.

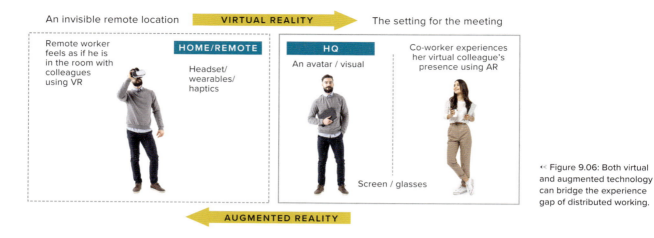

Figure 9.06: Both virtual and augmented technology can bridge the experience gap of distributed working.

The second question is what technological adaptations will be required to manage a hybrid work model where an increasing percentage of attendees will not be co-located? And taking into account the possibility that the current communication channel of video calls prevails, then dedicated cameras, microphones and interfaces for each attendee in the meeting become desirable, rather than grouping all physical attendees into a single frame. Meeting-room technology infrastructure will need to evolve to reflect this.

Perhaps the most challenging and profound question is how augmented and virtual reality will be used across all meetings. The technological and operational aspiration is likely to converge on a model where remote meeting participants can be inserted seamlessly into the physical fabric of the meeting by augmenting the experience of physical attendees. The empty chair opposite will become occupied by a photorealistic version of the remote attendee, through the modification of your own perception. Meanwhile the remote attendee will be able to live the experience of being in the room using virtual reality. In achieving this, the barriers and inconveniences of distributed meetings would be significantly ameliorated.

CONCLUSION

This end state will not be delivered overnight, and in the meantime the significant inconveniences of a mixed-mode collaboration model will likely determine behaviours. If everyone has individual choice on which days to collaborate in person and which days to collaborate remotely, the orchestration of a critical mass for physical meetings becomes challenging. In practice therefore, rather than individual flexibility, the future could lie in collective agreements on which days to be in the office and which not. On a systemic level we are already seeing the result of this taking the form of a mid-week peak in office use, with Mondays and Fridays increasingly consigned to home working.

Finally, the new technological requirements of the office now also translate to the home office. In the pandemic, many employers provided equipment to enable home working. As the mode of working becomes more complex, so will the cost of the technology, either leaving another bill to be paid by the employer or creating workforce inequalities between those who can afford their own interfaces and those who cannot.

LEARNING POINTS

- Technological augmentation is a constant throughout human history and has been one of the primary sources of economic and societal growth.

- The invention and evolution of the computer and the internet have radically reshaped the nature of work over the past 50 years.

- As digital technologies have developed, a key focus has been on making the virtual-physical interface more ergonomic. What started with switches now takes the form of rich virtual environments. The future emphasis will be on creating increased fidelity with the real world.

- Digitalisation of work has removed many physical artefacts from the workplace, such as filing cabinets and L-shaped desks. However, the need for monitors has increased in recent years and significantly shapes the function of many modern workplaces.

- Buildings themselves are becoming more intelligent, hastened by safety management during the pandemic. By digitising building operations, harvested data can be used predictively to better meet worker needs and to become more energy- and operationally efficient.

- Whereas recent speculation around metaverses offers a tantalising glimpse into the future, closed virtual environments will have much greater practical application and impact on the workplace in the coming years.

- New hardware will be developed that allows for less intrusive and visible interfaces. At some point this might include physical and neural implants. However, in the nearer term we should anticipate increased use of wearables and untethered screens.

- It is likely that at least a proportion of today's tasks and roles will be fully virtualised in the coming years. The nature and extent of these roles will vary significantly by industry and functional activity.

- Augmented and virtual reality will play an increasing role in all work interactions and offer the potential to provide a new bridge between physically co-located and remote workers.

CHAPTER 10

Ecosystems, communities and placemaking

INTRODUCTION

Work and community have long been intertwined. Centuries ago, people worked in the communities in which they lived. Mixed-use city centres formed bustling ecosystems, anchored by cultural and community venues such as churches, town halls, marketplaces and public houses.

However, with globalisation these ecosystems were supplanted. Workers travelled to cities to work and returned home to suburbs. Businesses sought customers overseas, rather than on their doorstep. Communities constructed around local synergies became dormitory suburbs and mono-cultural CBDs.

Covid-19 pushed a mass adoption of hybrid working and forced us to re-evaluate the role of community. The basis for human connection is rooted in our biology and our evolutionary need to be included. There is an abundance of academic research that links the lack of social connection to mental health disorders and poor quality of life. Community is at the heart of civilisation and central to happiness and survival.

COMMUNITY AND PLACE

Place contextualises community. The scale of place informs the nature of communities that develop there. People in small, isolated settlements tend to develop deep community ties with a small number of people, whereas people who live in large cities tend to create looser connections with a larger number of people and 'familiar strangers'.[1]

Whereas neither of these is objectively 'better', anthropological research estimates that the optimal community size is about 150 people, with a personal network being optimised at approximately 50 people.[2] Other studies have shown that people who live in high population densities are less happy.[3] Hence as more and more of us live in large cities and work for larger organisations our ability to network diminishes. Most of the friends we make in adulthood are from work (making friends at work is second only to making them in high school); it is at work that we come together to share common interests. So what happens now as work becomes untethered to place and we start to reduce the frequency with which we are physically together?

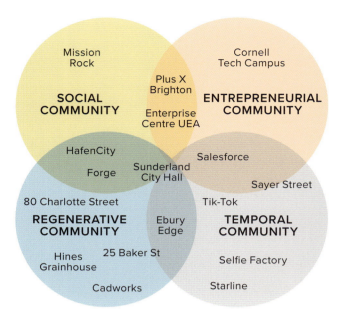

Figure 10.01: Four modern work communities

Physical attributes also shape communities. Amenities such as parks and leisure venues, football pitches and coffee shops provide the vehicles in which community collisions develop. Their structures confer symbolism and shape community, as workplaces do.

As hybrid working has multiplied the possibilities of work, so the communities in which workers interact have become more varied. Four modern work community typologies can be proposed:

Social Community

The boundaries of the workplace and its surrounding amenities have become porous. Workers thrive on deliberate engagement with external communities.

People used to come into offices because they had to. Now people come into town to work but also to engage in the broader spectrum of activities that city centres offer. In this context external amenities and places to build meaningful communities with others become an important component of the office worker's value proposition.

A study assessed over 12 submarkets in four US cities found that neighbourhoods that feature live-work-play amenities have experienced a higher return-to-office rate than office-dominated CBDs. In fact, vibrant, mixed-use exurbs showed greater performance than some urban neighbourhoods.[4]

Entrepreneurial Community

The strength of a business comes through a connected ecosystem of suppliers, customers and competitors. Chapter 6 considered how agglomerative communities add value to place and tend to be formed as communities of mutual interest. This is particularly the case for entrepreneurial communities which focus on small or start-up, creative, technology and science-based occupiers. In contrast to more mature agglomerations, entrepreneurial communities feature fast growth and fast fail-and-restart businesses. This dynamic environment relies on a high volume of shared information, transferable labour and mutual support. Entrepreneurial communities rely not only on purposeful placemaking but also on creative programming and community outreach.

Temporal Community

Not all communities need to be enduring. Experience or project-specific communities can drive value as a catalyst for innovation or regeneration.

Large-scale development projects can take a decade to plan and deliver. In the meantime, the affected city quarters can be left to stymie. Modern placemaking strategies address this through the creation of 'meanwhile uses' and other activation activities. This helps to give a sense of place, provide hints as to the future brand of the place and to provide a social nexus for local communities to engage in otherwise forgotten and excluded spaces. The communities that form around these 'meanwhile uses' may transition into both permanent work and social communities over time. Some act as a bridge to the future.

A balance needs to be found between creating new opportunities and retaining that which makes a place special. Temporal communities help to avoid 'wiped clean' gentrification.

Regenerative Community

As uses shift and places take on new purposes, the galvanisation and custodianship of new communities generate both economic and social benefits.

As the work model shifts and sustainability standards increase, the rate of obsolescence in yesterday's office stock is anticipated to rise significantly. In previous industrial shifts, economic obsolescence has created challenges for both communities and the physical fabric of cities. In the same way that factories of the industrial era gave way to the lofts of the service economy, new uses will be found for outdated offices.

This transformation is already under way in the retail sector, where we can see high-quality, well-located high streets and shopping centres pivot from transactional to experiential retail. Meanwhile many secondary retail assets are being repurposed for residential uses. Retailers such as the John Lewis Partnership are finding new uses for underutilised upper retail floors, such as residential and flex offices.

The bigger challenge for both society and the real estate sector is to establish, manage and curate the new communities that emerge from the ashes. Increasingly as master developers take longer-term custodianship roles in the sites they deliver, and as they are judged by their own stakeholders on ESG criteria, well-considered investments in placemaking and community creation are critical.

SOCIAL COMMUNITY EXAMPLES

CASE STUDY 10.01

Mission Rock

LOCATION: SAN FRANCISCO, USA

ARCHITECTS: WORKac, STUDIO GANG AND HENNING LARSEN

DEVELOPERS: TISHMAN SPEYER AND SAN FRANCISCO GIANTS

COMPLETION: 2025

Mission Rock positions community development as a catalyst for driving purposeful placemaking in a relatively undefined area of the city. Reconnecting the Mission Bay neighbourhood to the rest of San Francisco has provided an opportunity to create a vibrant new place with real community density.

Taking the lead from the San Francisco Giants baseball organisation and its strong roots in the community, developer Tishman Speyer approached the 11-hectares mixed-use development with a focus on site-specific design. Due to open by 2025, the site includes 8 acres of public space, 283 homes, 4,645 square metres of office space and an assortment of amenities.

Together, Tishman Speyer and the Giants sought out firms who would 'listen, be interested in learning from one another and be excited about going through a collaborative process'. This consortium of firms came together to build a masterplan sensitive not only to the future purpose of the site but connected with the surrounding existing context and communities.

The development has five core design goals:

1. Design the ground plane to connect blocks and expand the public realm
2. Make podiums into 'Mesas' that enliven their surroundings
3. Organise and shape towers to optimise views and create a memorable, collective silhouette
4. Respond to the Bay Area's climate and ecosystem to create a comfortable and sustainable environment
5. Select materials to tie the buildings and neighbourhood together.

Mission Rock features blocks that alternate between residential and commercial use. Studio Gang's Parcel F Tower combines housing, food, retail and co-working outlets across an activated ground plane that serves as the central social hub of the neighbourhood. WORKac's Block B office building draws the community upward through a series of balconies which function as outdoor modular meeting rooms, with a range of seating and greenery. For businesses with workplaces on the site, this is an integral element, providing the kind of variety which enables workplace ecosystems to thrive.

At a human scale, the ground floor of Block B is designed to extend the public realm into the building. The series of retail outlets and seating areas invite members of the public to interact with the building – creating a dynamic street-life.

We want to create a neighbourhood that has a genuine experience. Where a worker can go outside and engage socially in a way that wasn't setup by their employer. Real places where people aren't told what to do and how to do it.

MATT BISS, TISHMAN SPEYER

Figure 10.02: Studio Gang's Parcel F at Mission Rock will provide public terraces which wrap around the lower levels of the 23-storey building.

↱ Figure 10.03: The ground-floor retail outlets of Parcel F spill out on to public green space.

⤋ Figure 10.04: Parcel F's spacious tiered terraces

CHAPTER 10: ECOSYSTEMS, COMMUNITIES AND PLACEMAKING

◂◂ Figure 10.05: WORKac designed Block B's terraces to accommodate a range of activities.

▾ Figure 10.06: Block B maximises the view on to the central green space.

Figure 10.07: Block B from street level

Figure 10.08: WORKac's plans for the outdoor meeting rooms at Block B

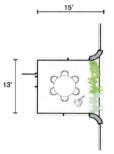

A: Small meeting room

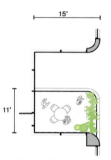

B: Small lounge

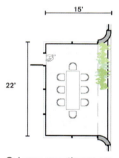

C: Large meeting room

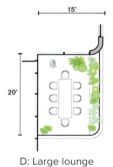

D: Large lounge

E: Double lounge

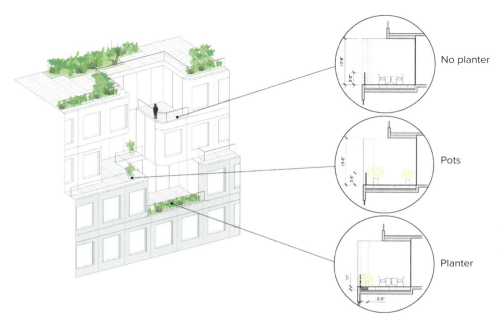

Figure 10.09: The planting strategy for Block B is designed to create variation and to accommodate differing levels of sunlight.

CHAPTER 10: ECOSYSTEMS, COMMUNITIES AND PLACEMAKING

CASE STUDY 10.02
25 Baker Street

LOCATION: LONDON, UK

ARCHITECT: HOPKINS ARCHITECTS

DEVELOPER: DERWENT LONDON

COMPLETION: ESTIMATED 2025

Figure 10.10: Derwent London's 25 Baker Street is due to open in 2025.

At 25 Baker Street, developer Derwent has activated the ground floor of its 27,600-square-metre mixed-use scheme. The mix of offices, retail and residential is set around a new landscaped courtyard, complemented by shopping streets, eating places and green spaces.

The 10-storey office building will offer 19,138 square metres of flexible workspace and a Skyroom amenity for all occupiers.

CASE STUDY 10.03

80 Charlotte Street

LOCATION: LONDON, UK

ARCHITECT: MAKE ARCHITECTS

DEVELOPER: DERWENT LONDON

COMPLETION: 2020

With the aim of enhancing user well-being, developer Derwent partnered with architecture studio Make to deliver its first major hybrid workplace post-pandemic. Designed to repurpose the existing building, the scheme is almost net zero in operation and made to be all-electric. The mixed-use scheme, including 4,180 square metres of residential units and ground-floor retail, is in the heart of London's creative district. The building's three atria bring natural light into the nine floors while a communal roof terrace and a public pocket park provide opportunities for people to work, relax and socialise out of doors. The ground floor has been designed to add to the animated streetscape, with a mix of retail units including a social space with a cafe open to the public, and operates as a space for occupiers to meet clients and host events.

Engineering company Arup is headquartered at 80 Charlotte Street, where it has created an app to measure indoor air quality and workplace occupancy. The app is sensor-driven and produces a live data stream and dashboards. The system enables Arup to monitor space use and occupancy day by day as well as track data over time, supporting ongoing efficient space management.

Figure 10.11: 80 Charlotte Street – a roof terrace with views over London

CHAPTER 10: ECOSYSTEMS, COMMUNITIES AND PLACEMAKING

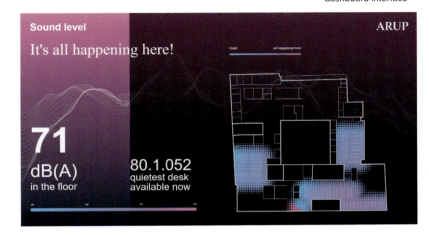

◂◂ Figure 10.12: The Arup dashboard

▾ Figure 10.13: Arup's dashboard interface

▾ Figure 10.14: The ground-floor social space and cafe at 80 Charlotte Street

ENTREPRENEURIAL COMMUNITY EXAMPLES

CASE STUDY 10.04

Plus X Brighton

LOCATION: BRIGHTON, UK

ARCHITECT: STUDIO EGRET WEST

COMPLETION: 2020

Plus X sits at the heart of a new mixed-use community. In partnership with Brighton & Hove City Council and the University of Brighton, regeneration specialist U+I worked with architect Studio Egret West to reimagine the area as a modern innovation quarter.

The genesis of Plus X began with the question 'what does it mean for workspace to be at the heart of a place?' The innovation hub was the first element to open and, despite launching just a few months into the pandemic, it was immediately full each month thanks to local businesses craving a sense of connection.

It has a welcoming and permeable ground floor which will be the social hub of the development – ultimately to include 380 homes, university buildings, student accommodation and a medical centre. This is achieved through the placement of a public route running straight through the centre of the building, with a cafe and event space.

Plus X provides small businesses with the tools and services they need to grow: workspace, specialist facilities, media suites, and a prototyping workshop with 3D printers and a Fabrication Laboratory.

One of the most attractive offerings to members is access to the Brighton Research Innovation Technology Exchange (BRITE) delivered in partnership with the University of Brighton, which provides tutorials, workshops and clinics with professional service partners. Offering a more holistic form of support is the resident yoga teacher who, as a human behaviour specialist, supports members in enhancing their mental resilience.

Café Domenica, a local charity, trains people with learning disabilities, offering young adults the opportunity to enhance their skills in a safe environment. Similarly, Creative Process, a local partner, reaches out to members to help place local apprenticeships.

⌃ Figure 10.15 (top): Plus X Brighton – spaces for casual collaboration

⌃ Figure 10.16: Members using a state-of-the-art media suite

▸▸ Figure 10.17: A roof terrace offers a change of scene.

◂◂ Figure 10.18: Café Domenica

▸▸ Figure 10.19: Workshops for the makers and inventors

CASE STUDY 10.05

Cornell Tech Campus

LOCATION:	EAST RIVER, NEW YORK
ARCHITECT:	SKIDMORE, OWINGS & MERRILL
DEVELOPER:	FOREST CITY RATNER CORPORATION
COMPLETION:	2017

Located in New York City's East River area, between Manhattan and Queens, Roosevelt Island's Cornell Tech campus was developed as the centre of the government's strategy for the expansion of the city's high-tech sector, in the hope of making New York City the capital of technological innovation. Since its opening, Cornell Tech has revived the island from its historical use as a prison, lunatic asylum and hospital to a vibrant and lively new campus and innovation hub. Amongst other accomplishments, the campus has graduated 1,200 tech alumni, launched more than 80 start-ups, raised nearly $1 billion in funding and increased the number of women pursuing computer science.[5]

Home to some of the US's biggest net zero emission buildings, the campus was built with sustainability as one of its key pillars, making it one of the most energy-efficient in the world. The House is the largest residential Passive House in the world, designed to save 882 tons of CO_2 per year.[6] A central utility plant that includes renewable sources provides energy to the campus.

Figure 10.20: Aerial view of Roosevelt Island, New York

Figure 10.21: Green public space as part of the Cornell Tech campus

CHAPTER 10: ECOSYSTEMS, COMMUNITIES AND PLACEMAKING

Figure 10.22: Views of the New York city skyline from Roosevelt Island

TEMPORAL COMMUNITY EXAMPLES

CASE STUDY 10.06
Sayer Street

LOCATION: ELEPHANT AND CASTLE, LONDON, UK

ARCHITECT: JAN KATTEIN ARCHITECTS

Sayer Street in south London activates a four-metre-wide temporary high street set against the construction hoarding of the masterplan. An established and thriving street, embedded in a community that otherwise would have faced a blank plywood wall, plays host to a lively and engaging cultural experiment with low-cost opportunities for local pop-ups and community entrepreneurs. This temporary architecture is as much a test lab for future permanent structures and services as it is about creating opportunities for urban life to flourish in transitional spaces.

Figure 10.23: Sayer Street, London – an example of temporary urbanism

CASE STUDY 10.07
Ebury Edge

LOCATION: LONDON, UK

ARCHITECT: JAN KATTEIN ARCHITECTS

When the Ebury Bridge Estate began to be redeveloped, Westminster City Council developed a 'temporary terrace of affordable workspaces, a cafe and a community centre to provide a continuous place for residents old and new to meet'. Working closely with local residents, the architects were able to design a brief reflecting how the community relates to its location. From workspaces sized to provide an affordable foothold for small local businesses to micro shopfronts, the space directly reflects and preserves the DNA of the surrounding community.

Figure 10.24: Ebury Edge temporary space was created to preserve displaced urban environment and community.

CHAPTER 10: ECOSYSTEMS, COMMUNITIES AND PLACEMAKING

REGENERATIVE COMMUNITY EXAMPLES

CASE STUDY 10.08
HafenCity

LOCATION: HAMBURG, GERMANY

MASTERPLAN: VARIOUS

ARCHITECT: VARIOUS

COMPLETION: ONGOING

Not just one of Europe's largest inner-city regeneration projects, HafenCity Hamburg (HCH) is also a living laboratory of contemporary urban development. Features in this docklands transformation include high-quality buildings and a generous public realm, energy-efficient heating, noise-reducing windows, excellent public transport to almost dispense with car use, a flood-protection system, a university, an opera house, a cruise terminal and a high proportion of affordable housing. The vision is for a new and exemplary city district providing 7,800 homes, 45,000 jobs – 35,000 of which will be in offices – and more than 2.5 million square metres of gross floor area above ground.

The development benefits from its attractive waterfront location, where historic industrial buildings sit alongside the new. The former dockland spans more than three kilometres from east to west as a series of islands in the River Elbe. Regeneration was sparked in the 1990s by advances in container shipping that required modern dock facilities; the scheme has helped to fund the construction of the new port, new infrastructure and the cost of the development team. The fall of the Berlin Wall also saw Hamburg strengthen its strategic location.

One of the keys to pursuing the ambitious vision and maintaining the high quality of the scheme has been its innovative governance and self-financing model. The governance aspect sees the land-holding HCH development company as master developer, while the self-financing mechanism stands in contrast to other large European dockland developments.

Figure 10.25: The masterplan of HafenCity, Hamburg

163

'The approach has been helped by the fact that the city owned most of the harbour and acquired additional land bringing it to 98 per cent ownership. Then funds were raised not by selling land, but by selling the right to develop which makes it possible to control quality,' explains Professor Jürgen Bruns-Berentelg, CEO of the HCH development company.

Bruns-Berentelg believes that incorporating specific features and technology has been at the expense of around 30% of income for HCH. However, the flipside of this experiment is that the project is widely recognised for its excellence in build quality and the public realm, and has attracted the best developers and architects. It has also drawn businesses, residents and tourists to this lively new waterside city.

Financing: The entire development area of HafenCity is under the ownership of the City of Hamburg, which named HCH its trustee. HCH is the master developer and finances all the elements of public infrastructure (roads, bridges, parks, social and cultural developments) from land proceeds. The private sector develops individual projects and follows regulatory requirements laid out by the city.

Planners/contractors: HCH is the master developer. For individual projects, HCH enforces a strictly competitive bidding process for building sites, reflecting 70% concept and 30% price. 700 architects have participated in the masterplan development.

Environmental and sustainability strategies: HCH evaluates the proposals of all prospective developers and architects against its own Ecolabel, which looks beyond energy performance. The sustainability strategies include a fine-grained mixture of uses, a high degree of walkability, excellent public transport (subway line and fuel-cell buses) and district heating with 92% renewable energy. All certification is above standard.

Energy sources: HafenCity Hamburg relies on clean thermal and geothermal energy as well as on different district heating systems.

Figure 10.26: HafenCity, Hamburg – the waterside public realm

CHAPTER 10: ECOSYSTEMS, COMMUNITIES AND PLACEMAKING

CASE STUDY 10.09

Dublin Docklands

LOCATION: DUBLIN, IRELAND

DEVELOPMENT AUTHORITY: DUBLIN DOCKLANDS DEVELOPMENT AUTHORITY

MASTERPLAN: DDDA WITH VARIOUS ARCHITECTS

COMPLETION: ONGOING

This extensive docklands redevelopment was initiated at the end of the last century to transform 520 hectares of derelict land close to the city's business district, and to attract inward investment that would reposition the city as a vibrant European centre for financial services and tech industries. Big names located their European headquarters there, including PwC, O2, CitiGroup, KPMG and Bank of New York along with Google, LinkedIn, Airbnb, TikTok and Facebook.

The area was designated a special economic zone (SEZ) called the International Financial Services Centre (IFSC). A masterplan was drawn up and investment levers were devised, with SEZ status delivering corporation tax incentives and Section 25 certificates making it possible for developers to bypass the planning system and secure permission often within a month.

Three phases are now complete. The first responded to the demand for modern office space but provided few amenities for workers. Phase 2 followed with mixed-use development, again with generous office accommodation. Most recently the third phase has incorporated residential units and offices, with the emphasis on high quality and excellent sustainability standards, supported by retail, restaurants and varied amenities including a world-class 2,100-seater theatre/opera house.

In all, so far, the regeneration has delivered more than 40,000 jobs and 11,000 new homes – 2,200 of which are affordable social housing.

⌃ Figure 10.27: Aerial overview of Dublin Docklands

⌄ Figure 10.28: Activation spaces along the River Liffey

CASE STUDY 10.10
Forge

LOCATION:	WOKING, UK
ARCHITECT:	HAWKINS\BROWN
DEVELOPER:	V7
COMPLETION:	2021

Forge is a workplace prioritising collaboration and amenity. This retrofitted 1990s office building features a redesigned central atrium which brings in natural light and introduces shared collaboration spaces that connect vertically and horizontally through the building. This infill is demountable and reconfigurable to suit changing occupier needs.

Along with studios and a cafe, these playful spaces support the predominantly creative occupiers and provide a range of alternative working environments throughout the day. Additionally, the basement level is home to a multi-use fitness studio, changing rooms and bike storage – which users can cycle directly into via a ramp in the reception area.

Figure 10.29: The collaboration spaces

Figure 10.30: The Forge features a reconfigurable steel grid of collaboration spaces in the atrium.

Figure 10.31: Swings add a playful element to this workplace.

CHAPTER 10: ECOSYSTEMS, COMMUNITIES AND PLACEMAKING

CASE STUDY 10.11

BVN's Radical Adaptation

LOCATION: GLOBAL
ARCHITECT: BVN

BVN Architecture's concept of 'Radical Adaptation' takes a whole systems approach to integrating existing and new build elements with fresh solutions for old structures and services, celebrating communities and heritage and activating underutilised buildings. The following examples illustrate a variety of adapted building types:

◄ Figure 10.32: Quay Quarter Tower, Sydney: 3XN developed in partnership with BVN – transforming a building at the end of its life by adding an additional 45,000 square metres, with demountable floor plates, while retaining 65% of the original structure

▲ Figure 10.33 (top): Stockland HQ, Sydney: BVN – redesigning a conventional building to increase its sustainability performance

▲ Figure 10.34: Queen & Collins Melbourne: BVN – transforming the future by paying tribute to historic heritage and blending the public and private realms

167

REWORKING THE WORKPLACE

→ Figure 10.35: Greenland Centre Sydney, BVN in association with Woods Baggot – redefining the open-air possibilities for residential skyscrapers with an additional 40 storeys while celebrating and giving back to the community with a state-of-the-art creative hub for rehearsals and productions on the ground floor

⌄ Figure 10.36: The innovation in residential skyscrapers is in the verandas, which have angled panes of glass, suspended from hand-like clips, prioritising views over the city and allowing for access to fresh air all the way to the top – which is a first at this height

CHAPTER 10: ECOSYSTEMS, COMMUNITIES AND PLACEMAKING

CASE STUDY 10.12

Sunderland City Hall

LOCATION: SUNDERLAND, UK

ARCHITECT/MASTERPLAN: FAULKNERBROWNS ARCHITECTS

Sunderland was once known as one of the greatest ports in the world, but the city has seen a significant decline in recent times. Working with Sunderland City Council, a masterplan was developed by FaulknerBrowns with the aim of regeneration and creating the first carbon-neutral urban quarter in the UK. At the centre of the Riverside Sunderland masterplan lies the City Hall, one of the first buildings completed. Developed as a civic hub, the City Hall integrates council departments, enabling new ways of working for the workforce.

Masterplan

The council has put its focus on the revival of the city centre, developing a solution that allows residents to live, work and play within a new urban quarter. Through exhibitions, workshops and consultations, the community created a set of aspirations which have resulted in the development of Keel Square as a connective route; the City Hall and Culture House as anchor attractions; and the development of pedestrian- and cycle-only roads to reduce traffic in the CBD.

The building

Located at the heart of the city quarter, the City Hall brings together the building's working community and the wider city community. The building is made of glass with no 'front', only sides that blend into the surrounding environment. The ground floor is open to the public and opens into the public realm. With the limiting of vehicles, the CBD and Riverfront Sunderland will be both safer and greener.

An oxide-red steel staircase resides at the centre of the City Hall, creating a bridge across the building. The staircase was built by local labourers Beal Architectural, a former ship-building firm. At full capacity, the City Hall can accommodate 2,000 workers in an open layout focused mainly on collaboration and social spaces.

Figure 10.37: Aerial view of Riverside Sunderland

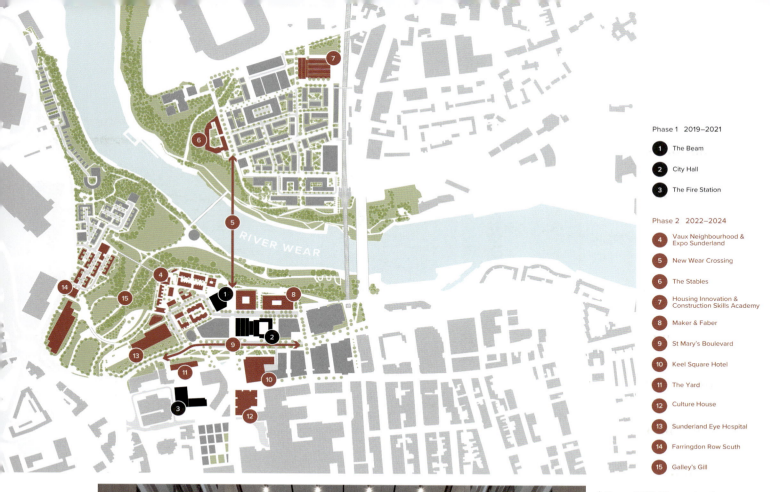

Figure 10.38: The masterplan for Riverside Sunderland

10.39: Seating under the central staircase in Sunderland City Hall's reception space

CHAPTER 10: ECOSYSTEMS, COMMUNITIES AND PLACEMAKING

Figure 10.40: A variety of workplace settings in Sunderland City Hall

Figure 10.41: Sunderland City Hall – alternative seating for casual collaboration

LEARNING POINTS

- Work and community are inextricably linked.
- Work is a fundamental driver of the value of place and the city.
- Work can now take place anywhere across an ecosystem of locations and places, aligning to the ESG agenda.
- Hybrid working has brought about a stronger bond to community and drawn attention to the role of place in supporting that bond.
- A good location is the starting point for success.
- Places with a purpose command higher values and occupancy.
- Reuse and repurpose are the new imperatives.
- The highest ESG credentials are now occupier expectations.
- Connect to the grid as part of a city-wide energy management network.
- Embed circular-economy design principles to reconfigure and reuse over time.
- Strong physical presence is required for landmarking and brand.
- Physically and virtually connect to local environments both internally and externally.
- Create a permeable ground floor with soft edges and subtle security lines.
- Provide a variety of shared amenity spaces with thoughtful experience management.
- Secure anchor tenants or features.
- Connect to nature with outdoor spaces, biophilia and well-designed public realms.
- Use data and user engagement to drive design and space management.

Conclusion

Office work has changed forever. The mass adoption of hybrid working and a re-evaluation of the concept of community bring challenges and opportunities for the workplace.

Work is a key engine of society, social inclusion, cities and buildings. And reshaping all of these is the internet, as it delivers radical change to the nature of working, shopping and living. It is breaking fundamental constructs such as knowledge, communications, presence, influence and trust, and is changing the nature of business. At a city level, the internet is dispensing with the penalties of distance on which urban economics are predicated. De-urbanisation and virtualisation will shift the composition of future cities towards distributed networks as well as rich, in-person experiences.

Society- and employee-led environmental, social and governance (ESG) priorities are drivers for how and where we work. The built environment must actively push net-zero targets and social justice or risk redundancy. To protect wider societies, developed Western nations may be called upon to pay reparations to developing countries who bear the brunt of climate disasters, or to go further than net zero with the offsetting of legacy carbon.

Meanwhile, the construction industry, building investors and occupiers need to collaborate across borders and with a common goal to reach carbon neutrality between 2030 and 2050. Industry and governments may continue to be slow to react, and this will likely result in the need for more drastic legislative changes in the near- to medium term while relying on self-imposed governance plans and certification accreditation to affect real change in the short term.

These are some of the changes we can see. Over the past 15 years many of the most economically impactful events, such as the global financial crisis, Brexit, the Covid-19 pandemic and the war in Ukraine, were either not predicted, or were predicted and considered

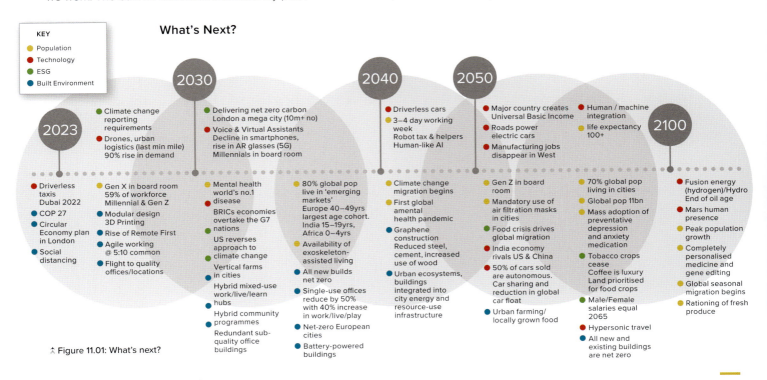

Figure 11.01: What's next?

unbelievable. One thing is certain, more major change is on its way; figure 11.01 looks to what's next, through the lenses of population, technology, ESG and the potential implications for the built environment.

PEOPLE

The pandemic has had a seismic impact on the power balance between employers and employees. The sentiment gap between junior and senior employees is wide. As younger generations progress through organisations, they are likely to drive more radical change by putting planet and people before profits. Organisations that support employees to connect to a purpose not only succeed in securing top talent, but also will reap increased productivity and innovation.

A proportion of today's tasks and roles will be virtualised in coming years. The nature and extent of these roles will vary by industry and activity. Work will be hybrid, balancing virtual and in-person teams and activities. Augmented and virtual reality will play an increasing role at work and create a new bridge between physically co-located and remote workers. With this growth will come the requirement for greater investment in technology and connectivity across workplaces and homes, as well as effective strategies to master self-agency and mental health.

Building a strong culture that encompasses the full ecosystem of work is central to the success of the future workplace. Despite the wealth of opportunities already created by this radical culture change, there is a risk that we become more individually focused and less collectivist. If this is not addressed, hybrid working could drive further social inequality between those afforded flexibility and balance and those who are not. However, while community and work remain inextricably linked, the role of physical place in maintaining community bonds is key.

Good health is re-established as central to work life, with the culture of well-being within organisations growing. Supporting vitality and positive mental wellness is key to facilitating engagement and productivity. Gender, physical abilities, age and life phases impact the need for alternative environments. Our bodies and brains are not static. What is required for effective cognitive and physical health is different at primary school compared to during retirement.

The metaverse offers a tantalising glimpse into the future, although in the near term expect closed virtual environments to have greater practical application and impact on the workplace. New hardware will be developed that allows for less intrusive and less visible interfaces, and, at some point, this may include physical and neural implants. We anticipate an increased use of wearables and untethered screens, perhaps including contact lenses. Integrating data management and predictive analytics (underpinned by neuroscience) will significantly shape how and where we work, live, relax and play.

PURPOSE AND REPURPOSE

The need to be together in person remains as strong as ever. Work and community are inextricably linked. The physical workplace is the social anchor for employees to bond, create, build culture and learn. This brings an increased focus on architecture and cities to create communities.

The purpose of place is evolving in an increasingly virtual world. As functional activities are automated and delivered remotely, the role of high-quality real estate needs to focus on higher-value activities. Physical place has a unique power to support brand values and inclusivity through designing for preferences driven by personality and neurodiversity. Buildings and places provide a sense of belonging and set the scene for memories.

The currency of experience is time. Workplace experience must be driven by user data and engagement. Data pools and occupier feedback will determine the best mix of uses, amenities and public realms across cities, campuses, high streets and homes. Services are delivered, but

CONCLUSION

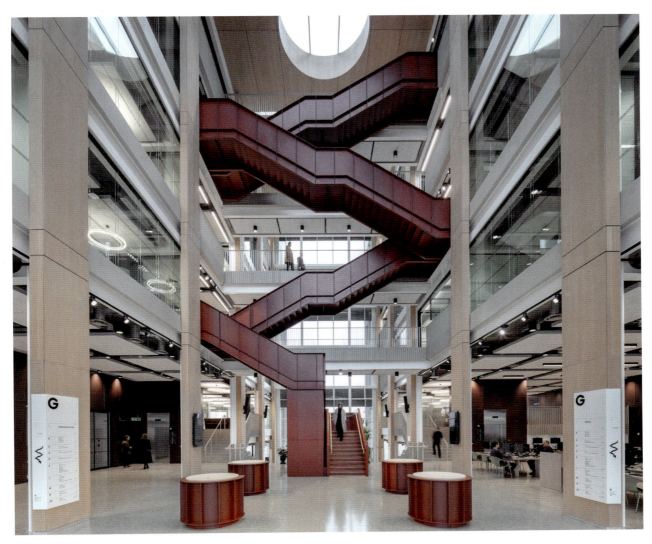

↑ Figure 11.02: Sunderland City Hall – internal connecting staircase (see chapter 10)

experiences are curated, which requires an evolution in building procurement and management.

Buildings need to shift from being carbon consumers to net-zero contributors and beyond, within a wider energy network and in support of community engagement. There are likely to be far fewer new buildings in the future as net-zero targets prioritise refurbishment and repurposing of existing stock as ways to offset carbon and to recontextualise cities to represent the inclusive needs of modern societies. As the climate crisis intensifies, buildings may need to address food sourcing, production and waste. Urban farming will increase with potential planning legislation requiring a natural environment or farming quota for building development.

175

Location and quality will determine whether a building is repurposed for the future or left to decay. There may come a tipping point when investors and occupiers prioritise carbon reduction over profit. In this case poorly located, designed, engineered and constructed buildings could be powered down and written off.

PLACE

Place contextualises community. Work is a fundamental driver of the value of place and of the city. Hybrid working has brought about a stronger bond to community and the role of place in supporting that bond. The power of community and human connection through place is a cornerstone of the future workplace. The successful design and management of workplaces will depend on a greater understanding of what it means to be human at work.

People derive value from place in four principal areas: amenity – shared facilities; agglomeration – the value of being part of an ecosystem; serendipity – the value of chance encounters; and ESG credentials – positive contributions to the physical and social environment.

Delivering a successful hybrid-working strategy requires organisations to consider all the components within an ecosystem and to establish an integrated delivery team consisting of facilities management, human resources, IT support, real estate, user representatives and members of trans-disciplinary professions such as psychologists and software engineers. Workplace experience blurs the boundaries between physical and virtual, further requiring this integrated approach.

While some office buildings will be left behind due to poor location or ESG credentials, others are at the forefront of change, already designed to net zero carbon targets and embracing social regeneration. The carbon challenge will require minimising embodied and operating carbon. This will need an integrated, data-driven approach between building investors, operators and occupiers.

Repurposing and reusing existing buildings, for community and experience, will be a priority for the building investment and development industry. High-quality buildings in great locations will retain value. The challenge is greater when it comes to reusing average-to-poor buildings in average-to-poor locations. Characteristics of buildings that will endure include being places with purpose; having a good location; possessing the highest ESG credentials; being physically and virtually connected; or being high-quality amenity spaces with great experience management and connections to nature.

This is a moment of pivotal change and those creating and managing workplaces have leapt to it with creativity, as long-held axioms have reshaped around them. Necessity is the mother of invention. However, this is not a step correction, nor is the hard work remotely finished. The change of course set in the past couple of years has an enduring glidepath that will dominate discussions on the workplace and the city for the next decade. During this time, external factors will not stand still. Notably, technology will continue to cut a disruptive path, forging new work models. The race will continue for the physical workplace to adapt. This is no time to rest. In the balance hangs productivity, worker satisfaction and real estate value. And perhaps as some of those reading this book run this race themselves, careers and world-changing agendas will open up in front of them.

As the late management consultant Peter Drucker once said, 'The best way to predict the future is to create it.'[1]

Notes

Introduction

1. Johann Hari, *Lost Connections: Uncovering the Real Causes of Depression – and the Unexpected Solutions*, Bloomsbury, London, 2018.

Chapter 1

1. Santo Milasi, Ignacio González-Vázquez and Enrique Fernández-Macías, 'Telework in the EU before and after the COVID-19: where we were, where we head to', *European Commission*, 2020, https://joint-research-centre.ec.europa.eu/system/files/2021-06/jrc120945_policy_brief_-_covid_and_telework_final.pdf (accessed 1 August 2022).
2. Cushman & Wakefield, insights from 'Experience per SF', aggregated from data across the UK and Europe, 2022, https://www.cushmanwakefield.com/en/united-states/services/global-occupier-services/total-workplace/experience-per-sf (accessed 23 September 2022).
3. Andrea Alexander, Aaron De Smet, Meredith Langstaff and Dan Ravid, 'What employees are saying about the future of remote work', McKinsey & Company, 2021, https://www.mckinsey.com/business-functions/people-and-organizational-performance/our-insights/what-employees-are-saying-about-the-future-of-remote-work (accessed 1 August 2022).
4. Laurel Farrer, 'The Art Of Asynchronous: Optimizing Efficiency In Remote Teams', 2020, https://www.forbes.com/sites/laurelfarrer/2020/12/10/the-art-of-asynchronous-optimizing-efficiency-in-remote-teams/?sh=46662a4c747c (accessed 1 August 2022).
5. Ashley Abramson, 'Burnout and stress are everywhere', American Psychological Association, https://www.apa.org/monitor/2022/01/special-burnout-stress (accessed 1 August 2022).
6. Susan Lund, Anu Madgavkar, James Manyika, Sven Smit, Kweilin Ellingrud, Mary Meaney and Olivia Robinson, 'The future of work after COVID-19', McKinsey & Company, 2021, https://www.mckinsey.com/featured-insights/future-of-work/the-future-of-work-after-covid-19 (accessed 1 August 2022).
7. World Economic Forum, 'The Future of Jobs Report', Centre for the New Economy and Society, 2018.
8. Despina Katsikakis, David Smith, Nicola Gillen, Antonia Cardone, Carol Wong, Bryan Berthold, Linsey Smith, Taylor van Dam and Rachel Casanova, 'Three New Realities Shaping Hybrid Workplace Strategies', Cushman & Wakefield, 2022, https://www.cushmanwakefield.com/en/insights/office-of-the-future-revisited (accessed 1 August 2022).
9. Aaron De Smet, Bonnie Dowling, Marino Mugayar-Baldocchi and Bill Schaninger, '"Great Attrition" or "Great Attraction"? The Choice is Yours', McKinsey & Company, 2022, https://www.mckinsey.com/business-functions/people-and-organizational-performance/our-insights/great-attrition-or-great-attraction-the-choice-is-yours (accessed 1 August 2022).
10. Ibid.
11. Mobility Matters Research, 'Peloton: One of 2020's best performers could repeat in 2021', Seekingalpha.com, https://seekingalpha.com/article/4398157-peloton-one-of-2020s-best-performers-repeat-in-2021 (accessed 24 November 2022).
12. World Health Organization, 'COVID-19 pandemic triggers 25% increase in prevalence of anxiety and depression worldwide', 2022, https://www.who.int/news/item/02-03-2022-covid-19-pandemic-triggers-25-increase-in-prevalence-of-anxiety-and-depression-worldwide (accessed 1 August 2022).
13. World Bank Group, 'Handbook for Gender-Inclusive Urban Planning and Design', 2020, https://www.worldbank.org/en/topic/urbandevelopment/publication/handbook-for-gender-inclusive-urban-planning-and-design (accessed 1 August 2022).
14. Nicola Gillen, *Future Office: Next-Generation Workplace Design*, RIBA Publishing, London, 2019.
15. Geert Hofstede, 'The 6 dimensions model of national culture', 2022, https://geerthofstede.com/culture-geert-hofstede-gert-jan-hofstede/6d-model-of-national-culture/ (accessed 1 August 2022).
16. Karen Stephenson, *The Quantum Theory of Trust: The Secret of Mapping and Managing Human Relationships*, Financial Times/Prentice Hall, 2004.
17. Anahita Baregheh, Jennifer Rowley and Sally Sambrook, 'Towards a multidisciplinary definition of innovation', *Management Decision*, vol. 47, issue 8, 2009, pp 1323–39.
18. Alexander S. Soldat, Robert C. Sinclair and Melvin M. Mark, 'Color as an Environmental Processing Cue: External Affective Cues Can Directly Affect Processing Strategy Without Affecting Mood', *Social Cognition*, vol. 15, issue 1, 1997, pp 55–71.
19. Dorothy A. Leonard and Sylvia Sensiper, 'The Role of Tacit Knowledge in Group Innovation', *California Management Review*, vol. 40, issue 3, 1998, pp 112–32.
20. Ibid.
21. Kate Morgan, 'Why in-person workers may be more likely to get promoted', BBC, 2022, https://www.bbc.com/worklife/article/20210305-why-in-person-workers-may-be-more-likely-to-get-promoted (accessed 1 August 2022).
22. Marco Dondi, Julia Klier, Frédéric Panier and Jörg Schubert, 'Defining the skills citizens will need in the future world of work', McKinsey & Company, 2021, https://www.mckinsey.com/industries/public-and-social-sector/our-insights/defining-the-skills-citizens-will-need-in-the-future-of-work (accessed 1 August 2022).
23. Paris Stevens, 'The 2021 Workplace Friendship & Happiness Survey', Wildgoose, 19 July 2019, https://wearewildgoose.com/usa/news/workplace-friendship-and-happiness-survey/ (accessed 1 August 2022).
24. Johann Hari, *Lost Connections: Uncovering the Real Causes of Depression – and the Unexpected Solutions*, Bloomsbury, London, 2018.

Chapter 2

1. Cushman & Wakefield, data aggregated from proprietary research tool 'Experience per SF'. Based on 185,000 respondents between 2020 and 2022, https://www.cushmanwakefield.com/en/united-states/services/global-occupier-services/total-workplace/experience-per-sf (accessed 23 September 2022).
2. Ibid.
3. Mary Barker, '4 Modes of Collaboration Are Key to Success in Hybrid Work', Gartner, 2021, https://www.gartner.com/smarterwithgartner/4-modes-of-collaboration-are-key-to-success-in-hybrid-work (accessed 23 September 2022).
4. Bonnie Dowling, Drew Goldstein, Michael Park and Holly Price, 'Hybrid work: Making it fit with your diversity, equity, and inclusion strategy', McKinsey & Company, 2022, https://www.mckinsey.com/business-functions/people-and-organizational-performance/our-insights/hybrid-work-making-it-fit-with-your-diversity-equity-and-inclusion-strategy (accessed 23 September 2022).
5. Cushman & Wakefield, proprietary research aggregated from 40 client projects between 2020 and 2022 across 11 European countries.
6. Cushman & Wakefield, insights from 'Experience per SF', aggregated from data across the UK and Europe, 2022, https://www.cushmanwakefield.com/en/united-states/services/global-occupier-services/total-workplace/experience-per-sf (accessed 23 September 2022).
7. Dana Rubinstein and Nicole Hong, 'As Remote Work Becomes Permanent, Can Manhattan Adapt?', *New York Times*, 12 April 2022, https://www.nytimes.com/2022/04/11/nyregion/remote-work-hybrid-manhattan.html?smtyp=cur&smid=tw-nytimes (accessed 23 September 2022).
8. Transport for London, 'Latest TfL figures show continued growth in ridership following lifting of working from home restrictions', 2022, https://tfl.gov.uk/info-for/media/press-releases/2022/february/latest-tfl-figures-show-continued-growth-in-ridership-following-lifting-of-working-from-home-restrictions (accessed 23 September 2022).
9. Cushman & Wakefield Research – CoreNet Global, 'Flexible Office in the Changing Workplace', 2022, https://cushwake.cld.bz/2022-Flex-Office-Changing-Workplace/2/ (accessed 29 September 2022).

Chapter 3

1. Joaquín Selva, 'What Is Self-Actualization? Meaning, Theory + Examples', Positive Psychology, 5 May 2017, https://positivepsychology.com/self-actualization/ (accessed 24 November 2022).
2. Health and Safety Executive UK, 'Sick building syndrome: Guidance for specialist inspectors', https://www.hse.gov.uk/foi/internalops/ocs/300-399/oc311_2.htm#:~:text=1%20Sick%20Building%20Syndrome%20(SBS,rather%20than%20a%20distinct%20illness (accessed 24 November 2022).
3. Nicola Gillen, *Future Office: Next-Generation Workplace Design*, RIBA Publishing, London, 2019.
4. Office for Health Improvement and Disparities, 'Important Findings', gov.uk, 2022, https://www.gov.uk/government/publications/covid-19-mental-health-and-well-being-surveillance-report/2-important-findings-so-far (accessed 19 July 2022).
5. David McDaid, 'Mental health problems cost UK economy at least £118 billion a year – new research', The London School of Economics and Political Science, 2022, https://www.lse.ac.uk/News/Latest-news-from-LSE/2022/c-Mar-22/Mental-health-problems-cost-UK-economy-at-least-118-billion-a-year-new-research (accessed 19 July 2022).
6. David B. Ross et al., 'Stress and its Relationship to Leadership and a Healthy Workplace Culture', in J.L. Bird and V.C. Bryan (eds), *Healthcare Community: Synergism Between Patient, Practitioners, and Researchers*, IGI Global, Hershey, PA, 2016, pp 161–93.
7. World Health Organization, 'Health and Wellbeing', 2022, https://www.who.int/data/gho/data/major-themes/health-and-well-being (accessed 19 July 2022).
8. Oxford English Dictionary, 'Well-being', Oxford English Dictionary, 2nd edn, 1989, https://www.oed.com/oed2/00282689;jsessionid=6C04BC77AD21CC7D7034E3096CDC0AD4#:~:text=The%20state%20of%20

being%20or,of%20a%20person%20or%20community) (accessed 19 July 2022).
9   World Health Organization, 'Measurement of and target-setting for well-being: an initiative by the WHO Regional Office for Europe', 2012, https://apps.who.int/iris/handle/10665/107309 (accessed 19 July 2022).
10 Caroline Criado Perez, *Invisible Women: Data Bias in a World Designed for Men*, Random House, London, 2019.
11 World Bank Group, 'Handbook for Gender-Inclusive Urban Planning and Design', 2020, https://www.worldbank.org/en/topic/urbandevelopment/publication/handbook-for-gender-inclusive-urban-planning-and-design (accessed 24 November 2022).
12 National Household Travel Survey, 'Trip Chaining', NHTS.gov, 2001, chrome-extension://efaidnbmnnnibpcajpcglclefindmkaj/https://nhts.ornl.gov/2001/pub/TripChaining.pdf (accessed 24 November 2022).
13 Mariam Arain et al., 'Maturation of the adolescent brain', *Neuropsychiatric Disease and Treatment*, vol. 9, 2013, pp 449–61, https://www.ncbi.nlm.nih.gov (accessed 19 July 2022).
14 Dimitri A. Christakis et al., 'How early media exposure may affect cognitive function: A review of results from observations in human and experiments in mice', *PNAS*, vol. 115, issue 40, pp 9851–58, https://www.pnas.org/doi/10.1073/pnas.1711548115 (accessed 19 July 2022).
15 Thuan-Quoc Thach, et al., 'Associations of perceived indoor environmental quality with stress in the workplace', *Indoor Air*, vol. 30, issue 6, 2020, pp 1166–77, https://doi.org/10.1111/ina.12696 (accessed 6 February 2023).
16 Gettysburg College, 'One third of your life is spent at work', 2017, https://www.gettysburg.edu/news/stories?id=79db7b34-630c-4f49-ad32-4ab9ea48e72b#:~:text=The%20average%20person%20will%20spend%2090%2C000%20hours%20at%20work%20over%20a%20lifetime (accessed 19 July 2022).

Chapter 4

1   C. Versace and M. Abssy, 'How Millennials and Gen Z are Driving Growth Behind ESG', *Nasdaq*, 2022, https://www.nasdaq.com/articles/how-millennials-and-gen-z-are-driving-growth-behind-esg (accessed 6 November 2022).
2   World Commission On Environment and Development, *Our Common Future*, Oxford University Press, Oxford, 1987.
3   https://unglobalcompact.org/what-is-gc/our-work/social.
4   United Nations Development Programme, 'United Nations Conventions Against Corruption', https://www.undp.org/lebanon/projects/united-nations-convention-against-corruption?utm_source=EN&utm_medium=GSR&utm_content=US_UNDP_PaidSearch_Brand_English&utm_campaign=CENTRAL&c_src=CENTRAL&c_src2=GSR&gclid=EAIaIQobChMI7M-gxuj4-wIVhO_tCh2mBAhpEAAYASAAEgI8dvD_BwE (accessed 15 October 2022).

Chapter 5

1   B. Joseph Pine II and James H. Gilmore, *The Experience Economy*, Harvard Business Review Press, Brighton, MA, 1999.
2   Cushman & Wakefield x WeWork, 'Flexible Office Is A Powerful Part of Your Workplace Strategy', 2022, https://www.cushmanwakefield.com/en/insights/flexible-office-is-a-powerful-part-of-your-workplace-strategy (accessed 27 September 2022).
3   Zappos, 'About Us', https://www.zappos.com/about/?utm_campaign=zappos&utm_medium=zappos-home&utm_source=footer&utm_content=text (accessed 2 February 2023).
4   Tony Hsieh, *Delivering Happiness: A Path to Profits, Passion, and Purpose*, Grand Central Publishing, New York, 2010.
5   Peter. F. Drucker, *Men, Ideas & Politics*, Harper & Row, New York, 1971.
6   Taiichi Ohno, *Toyota Production System: Beyond Large-Scale Production*, Productivity Press, 1988.
7   J. Myron Atkin and Robert Karplus, 'Discovery or Invention?', *The Science Teacher*, vol. 29, issue 5, 1962, pp 45–51.
8   Daniel Kahneman, Barbara L. Fredrickson, Charles A. Schreiber and Donald A. Redelmeier, 'When More Pain Is Preferred to Less: Adding a Better End', *Psychological Science*, vol. 4, issue 6, 1993, pp 401–405.

Chapter 6

1   Carmela Chirinos, 'Someone just paid $450,000 to be Snoop Dogg's neighbor in the metaverse. Here's how you can live by a celebrity too', Fortune, https://fortune.com/2022/02/02/how-to-buy-metaverse-real-estate-snoop-dogg-celebrity-neighbor/ (accessed 23 September 2022).
2   Ministry for the Development of the Russian Far East and Arctic, 'Far Eastern Hectare', https://web.archive.org/web/20210424013606/https://eng.minvr.ru/activity/razvitie-msp-i-konkurentsii/dalnevostochnyy-gektar/ (accessed 5 September 2022).
3   David Ricardo, *On the Principles of Political Economy and Taxation*, John Murray, London, 1817.
4   William Alonso, *Location and Land Use: Toward a General Theory of Land Rent*, Harvard University Press, New Haven, CT, 1964.
5   Paul Cheshire and Stephen Sheppard, 'On the Price of Land and the Value of Amenities', *Economica*, vol. 62, issue 246, 1995, p 247.
6   Office for National Statistics, 'Urban green spaces raise nearby house prices by an average of £2,500', 2019, https://www.ons.gov.uk/economy/environmentalaccounts/articles/urbangreenspacesraisenearbyhousepricesbyanaverageof2500/2019-10-14#:~:text=Public%20green%20space%20boosts%20the,expensive%20than%20those%20further%20away (accessed 7 September 2022).
7   Cushman & Wakefield, insights from proprietary statistical model 'RealSight' – based on data from the London market, 2022.
8   Battersea Power Station, 'The History', https://batterseapowerstation.co.uk/about/heritage-history/ (accessed 26 September 2022).
9   Emanuele Midolo, 'US Embassy relocation: was it a bad deal?', *Property Week*, 13 July 2018, https://www.propertyweek.com/features/us-embassy-relocation-was-it-a-bad-deal/5097656.article (accessed 26 September 2022).
10 Muse Marketing Strategy, 'Battersea Power Station', http://musestrategy.com/battersea-power-station-2/ (accessed 26 September 2022).
11 EL&N, 'EL&N London's most instagrammable place', https://elnlondon.com/ (accessed 5 September 2022).
12 Selfie Factory, 'The UK's First Instagram™ Inspired Funhouse', https://selfiefactory.co.uk/ (accessed 5 September 2022).
13 Cushman & Wakefield, 'Office of the Future Revisited', 2022, https://www.cushmanwakefield.com/en/insights/office-of-the-future-revisited (accessed 29 September 2022).
14 Chartered Institute of Personnel and Development, 'Organisational Culture and Cultural Change', 2020, https://www.cipd.co.uk/knowledge/culture/working-environment/organisation-culture-change-factsheet#gref (accessed 7 September 2022).
15 Magic Guides, 'Walt Disney World Statistics', https://magicguides.com/disney-world-statistics/ (accessed 26 September 2022).
16 Interbrand, 'Best Global Brands', https://interbrand.com/best-global-brands/ (accessed 26 September 2022).
17 Georgia Levenson, 'Disney (A): From Disneyland to Disney World, Learning the Art of Land Assembly', *Harvard Business Review*, 1997, https://store.hbr.org/product/disney-a-from-disneyland-to-disney-world-learning-the-art-of-land-assembly/898018 (accessed 26 September 2022).
18 Cliff Kuang, 'Disney's $1 Billion Bet on Magical Wristband', *Wired*, 18 March 2015, https://www.wired.com/2015/03/disney-magicband/ (accessed 26 September 2022).

Chapter 7

1   Barnet Council and Related Argent, 'Vision, A Park Town for Future London', Brent Cross Town, https://www.brentcrosstown.co.uk/vision (accessed 3 February 2023).
2   B.C. Wolverton, Anne Johnson and Keith Bounds, *Interior Landscape Plants for Indoor Air Pollution Abatement*, NASA and Sverdrup Technology, Bay Saint Louis, MS, 1989.
3   P.O. Fanger, *Thermal Comfort, Analysis and Applications in Environmental Engineering*, Danish Technical Press, Copenhagen, 1970.
4   'French supermarket tills where chit-chat is welcome grow in popularity', *The Connexion*, 5 February 2022, https://www.connexionfrance.com/article/French-news/French-supermarket-tills-where-chit-chat-is-welcome-grow-in-popularity (accessed 5 September 2022).

Chapter 8

1   Office for National Statistics, 'National Census and Registrar General's Mid-Year Population Estimates', *Public Intelligence*, http://www.manchester.gov.uk/download/downloads/id/25393/a20_1086-2016_manchester_population.pdf (accessed 2 August 2022).
2   Tertius Chandler, *Four Thousand Years of Urban Growth*, St. David's University Press, New York, 1987.
3   Dave Roos, 'How the East India Company Became the World's Most Powerful Monopoly', Sky History, 2020, https://www.history.com/news/east-india-company-england-trade (accessed 2 August 2022).
4   ONS, 'Employment in the UK: November 2022', https://www.ons.gov.uk/employmentandlabourmarket/peopleinwork/employmentandemployeetypes/bulletins/employmentintheuk/latest (accessed 2 August 2022).
5   Ibid.
6   'The opening of the Liverpool and Manchester Railway, 1830' *The Gazette*, https://www.thegazette.co.uk/all-notices/content/100741 (accessed 2 August 2022).
7   David Long, *TfL: The Story of the London Underground*, Bloomsbury, London, 2019.
8   Alan A. Jackson, *London's Metroland*, Capital Transport Publishing, Crowthorne, 2006.
9   'Historical Overview of London Population', London Online, https://www.londononline.co.uk/factfile/historical/ (accessed 2 August 2022).
10 John Rabon, 'London History: A Guide to Metroland – The Suburban Expansion of London brought on by the Tube', Londontopia, 2019, https://londontopia.net/history/london-history-a-guide-to-metroland-the-suburban-expansion-of-london-brought-on-by-the-tube/ (accessed 2 August 2022).
11 Paul E. Spector et al., 'A Cross-National Comparative Study of Work-Family Stressor, Working Hours and Wellbeing', *Personal Psychology*, vol. 57, issue 1, 2004, p 119.

12. Statista, 'Share of workers in the United States who check their work e-mails outside of normal work hours as of July 2019, by frequency', 2022, https://www.statista.com/statistics/911592/frequency-consumers-checking-work-emails-outside-work-hours/ (accessed 2 August 2022).
13. Joseph De Avila, 'New York City's Population Dips for First Time in Over a Decade', *Wall Street Journal*, 18 April 2019.
14. Rachel Botsman, *Who Can You Trust – How Technology Brought Us Together and Why It Could Drive Us Apart*, Penguin, London, 2017.
15. Robert J. Shiller, *Narrative Economics: How Stories Go Viral and Drive Major Economic Events*, Princeton University Press, Princeton, NJ, 2019.
16. European Commission, Directorate-General for Environment, *Reclaiming City Streets for People: Chaos or Quality of Life?*, European Commission Publications Office, 2004.
17. 'Rénovation, végétalisation: comment les Champs-Élysées vont se transformer', 2020, https://www.paris.fr/pages/les-champs-elysees-se-refont-une-beaute-21040 (accessed 2 August 2022).
18. Carlos Moreno et al., 'Introducing the "15-Minute City": Sustainability, Resilience and Place Identity in Future Post-Pandemic Cities', *Smart Cities*, vol. 4, issue 1, 2021, pp 93–111, https://www.mdpi.com/2624-6511/4/1/6 (accessed 2 August 2022).

Chapter 9

1. Frederick Winslow Taylor, *The Principles of Scientific Management*, Dover Publications, New York, 1998.
2. Ford, 'The Moving Assembly Line and The Five-Dollar Workday', https://corporate.ford.com/articles/history/moving-assembly-line.html (accessed 31 August 2022).
3. Mikey McGovern, 'Charles Babbage's Difference Engine', Explore Whipple Collections, https://www.whipplemuseum.cam.ac.uk/explore-whipple-collections/calculating-devices/charles-babbages-difference-engine (accessed 25 January 2022).
4. Ben Russell, 'Rebuilding Eric: UK's First Robot', Science Museum, 2016, https://blog.sciencemuseum.org.uk/rebuilding-eric-the-uks-first-robot/ (accessed 30 September 2022).
5. Gordon E. Moore, 'Cramming more components onto integrated circuits', *Electronics*, vol. 38, issue 8, 19 April 1965, pp 114 ff, https://newsroom.intel.com/wp-content/uploads/sites/11/2018/05/moores-law-electronics.pdf (accessed 25 August 2022).
6. Michael DeGusta, 'Are Smart Phones Spreading Faster than Any Technology in Human History?', *MIT Technology Review*, 9 May 2012, https://www.technologyreview.com/2012/05/09/186160/are-smart-phones-spreading-faster-than-any-technology-in-human-history/ (accessed 25 August 2022).
7. WiredScore, 'WiredScore: Setting the global standard for technology in the built world', https://wiredscore.com/ (accessed 7 September 2022).
8. Ted Moudis Associates, '2017 Workplace Report: TMA by the Numbers', 2017, https://static1.squarespace.com/static/5ed935eb838ffc6d44b0ebf3/t/5f32c387d4fed24a575d18f5/1597162380674/2017+TMA+Workplace+Report.pdf (accessed 7 September 2022).
9. Statista, 'Share of internet users worldwide using their mobile phone to make video calls in the past month as of 4th quarter 2021, by age and gender', 2022, https://www.statista.com/statistics/1254856/mobile-video-calling-age-gender-distribution/ (accessed 5 October 2022).
10. Guy Campos, 'Videoconferencing app usage "hits 21 times pre-Covid levels"', *Av Interactive Magazine*, 5 August 2021, https://www.avinteractive.com/news/collaboration/usage-mobile-video-conferencing-apps-including-zoom-grew-150-first-half-2021-05-08-2021/ (accessed 5 October 2022).
11. Polly.ai, 'State of Virtual Meetings 2021', https://www.polly.ai/hubfs/DLC%20Assets/The%20State%20of%20Virtual%20Meetings.pdf (accessed 5 October 2022).
12. Calendly, 'Calendly: Easy Scheduling Ahead', https://calendly.com/ (accessed 12 October 2022).
13. Gather, 'Gather: Build digital spaces for your distributed team to make virtual interactions more human', https://www.gather.town/ (accessed 7 September 2022).
14. 'Teamflow: The Remote Office for Extraordinary Teams', https://www.teamflowhq.com/ (accessed 12 October 2022).
15. Jason Lawrence et al., *Project Starline: A high-fidelity telepresence system*, Google Research, USA, https://storage.googleapis.com/pub-tools-public-publication-data/pdf/3696afb4c1cccbe0876a9fedd1586f0f9c84f737.pdf (accessed 20 July 2022).
16. Clay Bavor, 'Project Starline: Feel like you're there, together', Google Research Blog, 2021, https://blog.google/technology/research/project-starline/ (accessed 21 August 2022)
17. Computer History Museum, 'Atanasoff-Berry Computer', Computer History Museum Exhibition Birth of the Computer, https://www.computerhistory.org/revolution/birth-of-the-computer/4/99 (accessed 25 August 2022).
18. Trevor Wheelwright, '2022 Cell Phone Usage Statistics: How Obsessed Are We?', Reviews.org, 2022, https://www.reviews.org/mobile/cell-phone-addiction/ (accessed 5 October 2022).
19. Paul E. Spector et al., 'A Cross-National Comparative Study of Work-Family Stressors, Working Hours, and Well-Being: China and Latin America Versus the Anglo World', *Personnel Psychology*, vol. 57, issue 1, 2004, pp 119–142.
20. Mojo, 'Mojo Lens', https://www.mojo.vision/mojo-lens (accessed 7 September 2022).
21. AP, 'A Swedish start-up has started implanting microchips into its employees', CNBC, 2017, https://www.cnbc.com/2017/04/03/start-up-epicenter-implants-employees-with-microchips.html (accessed 7 September 2022).
22. Neuralink, 'Neuralink: Breakthrough Technology for the Brain', https://neuralink.com/ (accessed 7 September 2022).
23. Carolyn Giardina, 'Inside Construction of the MSG Sphere, the $1.8B Las Vegas Venue', *The Hollywood Reporter*, 24 May 2022, https://www.hollywoodreporter.com/business/business-news/msg-sphere-las-vegas-1235152882/ (accessed 10 October 2022).
24. MSG Sphere, 'MSG Sphere: Beyond a Venue', https://www.msgsphere.com/about (accessed 10 October 2022).
25. Clive Young, 'MSG Sphere's Immersive Sound Technology to Debut in New York', *MIX*, 26 July 2022, https://www.mixonline.com/live-sound/venues/msg-sphere-immersive-sound-beacon-theatre (accessed 10 October 2022).
26. Luke Dormehl, 'Who needs headphones? Holoplot can beam audio directly to your ears from afar', *digitaltrends*, 18 June 2021, https://www.digitaltrends.com/cool-tech/holoplot-beamforming-audio/ (accessed 10 October 2022).
27. SACO, 'MSG Spheres at the Venetian: a venue for the next generation of experiences', 2022, https://www.saco.com/msg/#:~:text=LED%20Media%20Plane,-SACO%20bespoke%20LED&text=Inside%2C%20MSG%20Sphere%20will%20house,of%20a%20high-definition%20television (accessed 10 October 2022).
28. 'The MSG Sphere: The Future of Live Concert Experiences', *Music Business Journal*, 2022, http://www.thembj.org/2018/11/the-msg-sphere-the-future-of-live-concert-experiences/ (accessed 10 October 2022).

Chapter 10

1. Stanley Milgram, 'The Familiar Stranger: An Aspect of Urban Anonymity', *The Division 8 Newsletter, Division of Personality and Social Psychology*, American Psychological Association, Washington DC, 1972.
2. R. I. M. Dunbar and Susanne Shultz, 'Evolution in the social brain', *Science*, vol. 3, issue 5843, 2007, pp 1344–7.
3. John V. Winters and Yu Li, 'Urbanisation, natural amenities and subjective well-being: Evidence from US counties', *Urban Studies*, vol. 5, issue 8, 2016, pp 1956–73.
4. Cushman & Wakefield, proprietary research aggregated from 12 submarkets across New York, Atlanta, Chicago and San Francisco comparing April–June 2019 and April–June 2022.
5. Cornell Tech, 'Cornell Tech Celebrates 10th Anniversary of Winning NYC Competition', 2021, https://tech.cornell.edu/news/cornell-tech-celebrates-10th-anniversary-of-winning-nyc-competition/ (accessed 18 Sept 2022).
6. The House at Cornell Tech, 'We've pulled out all the stops for sustainability. The House at Cornell Tech is the tallest and largest Passive House residential building in the world', https://thehouseatcornelltech.com/sustainability/ (accessed 18 Sept 2022).

Conclusion

1. Joe Maciariello, 'Joe's Journal, On Creating the Future', The Drucker Institute, 2011, https://www.drucker.institute/thedx/joes-journal-on-creating-the-future/ (accessed 3 February 2023).

Bibliography

Anthes, E., *The Great Indoors: The Surprising Science of How Buildings Shape Our Behavior, Health, and Happiness*, New York: Scientific American/Farrar, Straus and Giroux, 2020.

Breen, B. and Hollender, J., *The Responsibility Revolution: How the Next Generation of Businesses Will Win*, Chichester: John Wiley & Sons, 2010.

British Council for Offices, *Designing for Neurodiversity*, London: British Council for Offices, 2022.

Clack, A. and Gabler, J., *Managing Diversity and Inclusion in the Real Estate Sector*, Abingdon and New York: Routledge, 2019.

Cheshire, D., *The Handbook to Building a Circular Economy*, London: RIBA Publishing, 2021.

Coady, T., *Rebuilding Earth: Designing Ecoconscious Habitats for Humans*, Berkeley, CA: North Atlantic Books, 2020.

Conceicao, P., *Human Development Report 2019: Beyond Income, Beyond Averages, Beyond Today: Inequalities in Human Development in the 21st Century*, New York: UNDP, 2019.

Criado-Perez, C., *Invisible Women: Exposing the Gender Bias Women Face Every Day*, New York: Vintage, 2020.

Ellen MacArthur Foundation, 'Circular Economy Overview', 2017, https://www.ellenmacarthurfoundation.org/circular-economy/overview/concept.

Gates, B., *How to Avoid a Climate Disaster: The Solutions We Have and the Breakthroughs We Need*, New York: Alfred A. Knopf, 2021

Harari, Y.N., *21 Lessons for the 21st Century*, London: Vintage, 2019.

Hari, J., *Lost Connections: Uncovering the Real Causes of Depression – and the Unexpected Solution*, New York: Bloomsbury, 2018.

Jacobs, J., *The Death and Life of Great American Cities*, New York: Vintage, 1993.

Kern, L., *Feminist City: Claiming Space in a Man-Made World*, London: Verso, 2021.

Kotter, J.P., *A Sense of Urgency*, Boston, MA: Harvard Business School Press, 2008.

Ladau, E., *Demystifying Disability*, Emeryville, CA: Ten Speed Press, 2021.

Maslin, S., *Designing Mind-Friendly Environments: Architecture and Design for Everyone*, London: Jessica Kingsley Publishers, 2021.

Moss, J., *The Burnout Epidemic: The Rise of Chronic Stress and How We Can Fix It*, Boston, MA: Harvard Business Review Press, 2021.

Nelson, E. and Holzer, D., *The Healthy Office Revolution: A True Story of Burnout, a Wake Up Call and Better Working Through Science*, Learn Adapt Build Publishing, *2017.*

Polman, P. and Winston, A., *Net Positive: How Courageous Companies Thrive by Giving More Than They Take*, Boston, MA: Harvard Business Review Press, 2021.

Sailer K., Pomeroy, R. and Haslem, R., 'Data-Driven Design: Using Data on Human Behaviour and Spatial Configuration to Inform Better Workplace Design', *Corporate Real Estate Journal*, vol. 4, issue 3, 2015, pp 249–62.

Sternberg, E., *Healing Spaces: The Science of Place and Well-Being*, Cambridge, MA: Belknap Press of Harvard University Press, 2010.

Sternberg, E., *The Balance Within: The Science Connecting Health and Emotions*, New York: W.H. Freeman, 2000.

Taub, L. and Nall, J., *The Whipple Museum of the History of Science*, Cambridge: Cambridge University Press, 2019.

Thunberg, G., *The Climate Book*, London: Allen Lane, 2022.

Tarkett and HOK, 'Sensory Processing, Neurodiversity and Workplace Design, Research Report', 2022, https://contract.tarkett.com/neurodiversity.

UNDP (United Nations Development Programme), *Human Development Report 2021–22: Uncertain Times, Unsettled Lives – Shaping Our Future in a Transforming World*, New York, 2022, https://hdr.undp.org/content/human-development-report-2021-22.

Vince, G., *Nomad Century: How Climate Migration Will Reshape Our World*, New York: Flatiron Books, 2022.

Vischer, J.C., 'Towards an Environmental Psychology of Workspace: How People are Affected by Environments for Work', *Architectural Science Review*, vol. 51, issue 2, 2008, pp 97–108.

Index

A

AECOM 41–44, 103–105
agglomerations 89, 90
AHR Architects 107–109
Akira (movie) 128
Amazon Fresh 112
amenities 89–90
Architype 61–62
Arup 156–157
augmented reality 139, 142
Australia
    Sydney NGO Precinct and Social Enterprise Hub 63

B

25 Baker Street, London 155
Barr Gazetas 85
Battersea Power Station, London 93–94
BDG 68–70
bid rent theory 88
biomimetic design; *see* inclusive design
Bjarke Ingels Group 113–115
brain maturation 45
Brent Cross Town, London 101–102
Brundtland Report 56
Bruns-Berentelg, Jürgen 164
BVN Architecture 167–168

C

Caccioppo, John 19
Cadworks, Glasgow 60
CapitaSpring, Singapore 113
career networks 17–18
Carlo Ratti Associati 113–115
Carrefour 112
case studies
    entrepreneurial community 158–161
    experience destinations 101–102, 103–105, 107–109, 110–115
    fostering innovation 61–62
    hybrid working 24–26, 29, 32
    inclusive design 41–44, 46–53
    inclusivity and equity 63
    physical-virtual interface 138, 141
    regenerative community 163–171
    social community 150–157
    social resilience 64–65
    sustainable development 66–70
    sustainable economic growth 60
    temporal community 162
    value and purpose of place 91, 93–94
    well-being and nature 58–59
    workplace communities 16
    workplace culture 12–13
    workplace experience 77, 79, 81, 84–85
80 Charlotte Street, London 156–157
cities 120–131
    future 125–128
    history 120–122
    internet and 124–125
    reinvigorating 129–130
    today's challenges 122–124
climate change 64–65
contactless design 137
Cornell Tech Campus, New York, USA 160–161
Covid-19 pandemic, impacts of 8–20, 125
co-working spaces 15, 16, 28, 35, 66–67
culture, workplace 10–14, 130
Cushman & Wakefield
    Experience per Square Foot (XSF) tool 8, 10, 22, 24–26, 32
    hybrid meeting principles 30
    Living Lab, Utrecht 12–13

D

Derwent London 155, 156–157
de-urbanisation 124
Diageo 110–111
digital communities 20
diversity, equity and inclusion 11, 30–31, 63, 66–70, 83
Drucker, Peter F. 79
Dublin Docklands, Ireland 165

E

East India Company 120
Ebury Edge, London 162
economic growth, sustainable 60
electricity 121
employee power 10
Energy Supply Board (ESB), Dublin, Ireland 103–105
Enterprise Centre, University of East Anglia, Norwich 61–62
entrepreneurial community 149, 158–161
environmental, social and governance (ESG)
    performance 56
    see also social sustainability
Epicenter 141
equity; *see* diversity, equity and inclusion
evidence-based insight 11
experience destinations 100–115
    case studies 101–102, 103–105, 107–109, 110–115
    creating scaled experiences 110–115
    definition 100
    key principles 106
    purpose 103
    see also workplace experience
Experience per Square Foot (XSF) tool 8, 10, 22, 24–26, 32
expert knowledge networks 17
explicit knowledge 17
EZ Concept 110–111

F

facilities management (FM) 78
FaulknerBrowns Architects 169–171
15-minute cities 102, 121, 130
Five Whys Method 79, 80
5E customer experience model 80
flexible working 9, 129
    see also hybrid working
FORE Partnership 60
Forest City Ratner Corporation 160–161
Forge, Woking 166
'Four Realms of an Experience' model 80

G

gender and gender identification 45
Germany
    HafenCity Hamburg 163–164
Gilmore, Jim 76, 79, 80
Google Starline 138
Grafton Architects 103–105
Grainhouse, Covent Garden, London 85
Greenhalgh, Tim 78, 80
greening cities 129

H

HafenCity Hamburg, Germany 163–164
    HALO Enterprise and Innovation Centre (HEIC), Kilmarnock, Scotland 66–67
haptic immersion 141, 142
Hatton Garden, London 90
Hawkins\Brown 166
health and well-being 11, 38–40
    definitions 40
    dimensions of 39
    nature and 58–59
    objective and subjective well-being 19
    see also inclusive design
Henning Larsen Architects 150–154
hierarchy of needs 38, 95
Hines 85
HMRC 41–44

HOK 46–50
home working 8, 22–23
    see also hybrid working
Hopkins Architects 155
housing shortage 122–124
HqO 29
Huckletree, White City, London 16
human rights 57, 58–59
human-centric design; see inclusive design
hybrid meetings 30, 136
hybrid working 8–9, 10–11, 22–35, 148
    benefits 28
    case studies 24–26, 29, 32
    challenges 26–27
    co-working spaces and 35
    delivering 33–34
    diversity and inclusion 30–31
    impacts on neighbourhoods 34
    impacts on office space 32–33
    models 27–28
    organisational strategies 31–32
    realities 22–26
    technology 28–29, 34
    workplace experiences 83

I

inclusion; see diversity, equity and inclusion
inclusive design 40–54
    age and life phases 45
    case studies 41–44, 46–53
    gender and gender identification 45
    neurodiversity 46–50
individualism vs collectivism 14
indoor environmental quality (IEQ) 45
innovation networks 15
internet 20, 124–125
Ireland
    Dublin Docklands 165
    Energy Supply Board (ESB), Dublin 103–105

J

J&L Gibbons 59
Jaego's House, London 84
Jan Kattein Architects 162
Jencks, Maggie Keswick 51
Johnnie Walker, Princes Street, Edinburgh, Scotland 110–111

K

Keppie Design 110–111
King's College London 59
knowledge networks 17
Koninklijk Instituut voor de Tropen 64–65

L

Landor & Fitch 78, 79, 80
learning networks 19
Leesman Office Survey 29
Little Houses Group 84
Living Lab, Utrecht, Netherlands 12–13
location strategy trends 91

M

McKinsey 9, 10, 31
Madison Square Garden Sphere, Las Vegas, USA 141
Maggie's Centres 51–53
Make Architects 156–157
Maslow, Abraham 38, 95
measurement 11, 82
meeting-room technologies 137
meetings
    hybrid 30, 136
    video calling 29, 136, 137, 143–144
    virtual worlds 137–139
mental health issues 9, 11, 39–40, 58–59
metaverses 139, 142
Metro-land 122
Metropolis (movie) 128
Mission Rock, San Francisco, USA 150–154
Mojo Lens 140–141
movies, futuristic 128
Musk, Elon 141

N

nature
    well-being and 58–59
needs, hierarchy of 38, 95
Netherlands
    Living Lab, Utrecht 12–13
    SDG House, Amsterdam 64–65
network effects 124
networks 15–19
    career 17–18
    expert knowledge 17
    innovation 15
    learning 19
    social 19
    work 15
net-zero development 60, 66–67
neural implants 141, 142
neurodiversity 46–50
Nomad Projects 59

O

objective well-being 19
office space
    occupancy rates 26–27
    space allocation changes 32–33
O'Mahony Pike Architects 103–105
organisational culture; see workplace culture
organisational network analytics 15–19
Our Common Future 56

P

Parabola 110–111
Passive House 61–62, 160
peak-end rule 82
permitted use 92
physical-virtual interface 134–145
    blended human and digital experiences 78–79
    case studies 138, 141
    current workplaces 28–29, 135–137
    cutting-edge technologies 142
    future workplaces 29, 143–144
    history 134–135
    metaverses 29, 139, 142
    smart buildings 136–137
    smart people 140–142
    video calling 29, 136, 137, 143–144
    virtual worlds 29, 137–139
Pine, Joe 76, 80
planning controls 92
Plus X Brighton 158–159
predictive diary management 137
predictive resource allocation 137
'presence privilege' 31
Project Starline 138
property technology 29
psychophysics 19
public transport 92, 121, 122, 129

R

railways 121, 122, 129
regenerative community 149, 163–171
Related Argent 101–102
remote working 8–9, 27–28
    see also hybrid working
remote-first working 27–28
rent, theory of 88
resilience, social 64–65
Ricardo, David 88
Royal College of Physicians 107–109

S

safety elevator 121
Salesforce 32
Samuel, Harold 88
San Francisco Giants 150–154
Sayer Street, Elephant and Castle, London 162
SDG House, Amsterdam, Netherlands 64–65
Sea Containers House, South Bank, London 68–70

Selfie Factory, London 112
Singapore
    CapitaSpring 113–115
Singtel 79
Skidmore, Owings & Merrill 160–161
smart buildings 136–137
smart people 140–142
smartphones 140
social community 148–149, 150–157
social networks 19
social sustainability 56–71
    business case for 68
    healthy lives and human rights 58–59
    inclusivity and equity 63
    resilience and innovation 61–62
    social resilience 64–65
    socially sustainable communities 66–70
    sustainable economic growth 60
social value creation 68
spaceOS 29
The Spine, Royal College of Physicians, Liverpool 107–109
Stephenson, Karen 15
Studio Egret West 158–159
Studio Gang 150–154
Studio RHE 16
subjective well-being 19
suburbanisation 122, 124
'success-from-anywhere' approach 32
Sunderland City Hall 169–171
sustainability, social; *see* social sustainability
sustainable development 56–57, 66–70
Sustainable Development Goals (SDGs) 57
sustainable economic growth 60
Sydney NGO Precinct and Social Enterprise Hub, Australia 63

T

tacit knowledge 17
technology 9, 28–29, 134–145
    blended human and digital experiences 78–79
    case studies 138, 141
    current workplaces 28–29, 135–137
    cutting-edge 142
    delivering hybrid working 34
    digital communities 20
    future workplaces 29, 143–144
    history 134–135
    internet 20, 124–125
    metaverses 29, 139, 142
    smart buildings 136–137
    smart people 140–142
    social connections and 19
    video calling 29, 136, 137, 143–144
    virtual worlds 29, 137–139
temporal community 149, 162
theory of rent 88
Tikky Town, London 112
time as 'currency of experience' 76–77
Tishman Speyer 150–154
Toyota, Sakichi 79
Twain, Mark 88

U

UK Household Longitudinal Study (UKHLS) 39–40
United Kingdom
    25 Baker Street, London 155
    80 Charlotte Street, London 156–157
    Battersea Power Station, London 93–94
    Brent Cross Town, London 101–102
    Cadworks, Glasgow 60
    Ebury Edge, London 162
    Enterprise Centre, University of East Anglia 61–62
    FORE Partnership 60
    Forge, Woking 166
    Grainhouse, Covent Garden, London 85
    HALO Enterprise and Innovation Centre (HEIC), Kilmarnock 66–67
    Hatton Garden, London 90
    HMRC inclusive design 41–44
    Huckletree, White City, London 16
    Jaego's House, London 84
    Johnnie Walker, Princes Street, Edinburgh 110–111
    Maggie's Centres 51–53
    Plus X Brighton 158–159
    Sayer Street, Elephant and Castle, London 162
    Sea Containers House, South Bank, London 68–70
    Selfie Factory and Tikky Town, London 112
    The Spine, Royal College of Physicians, Liverpool 107–109
    Sunderland City Hall 169–171
    Urban Mind Project, King's Cross, London 58–59
United Nations Global Compact 57
United States
    Cornell Tech Campus, New York 160–161
    Madison Square Garden Sphere, Las Vegas 141
    Mission Rock, San Francisco 150–154
    Walt Disney World Resort, Florida 97
University of East Anglia, Norwich 61–62
Urban Mind Project, King's Cross, London 58–59
urbanisation 120, 124

V

V7 166
value and purpose of place 88–98
    agglomeration 89, 90
    amenity 89–90
    case studies 91, 93–94
    modern value models 92
    new purpose for place 95–97
    rent theory 89
    serendipity 89, 90
video calling 29, 136, 137, 143–144
Virgin Money 80–81
virtual receptionist 137
virtual worlds 137–139

W

Walt Disney World Resort, Florida, USA 97
well-being 11, 38–40
    definitions 40
    dimensions of 39
    nature and 58–59
    objective and subjective 19
    see also inclusive design
WeWork 35, 77
WilkinsonEyre 93–94
work networks 15
WORKac 150–154
working from home 8, 22–23
    see also hybrid working
work-life balance 9, 22–23, 122–124
workplace communities 14–19
    entrepreneurial community 149, 158–161
    regenerative community 149, 163–171
    social community 148–149, 150–157
    temporal community 149, 162
workplace culture 10–14, 130
workplace experience 76–86
    blended human and digital experiences 78–79
    case studies 77, 79, 81, 84–85
    delivering 79–83
    equitable 83
    'mechanics' and 'humanics' of 77–78
    time as 'currency of experience' 76–77
    see also experience destinations
World Bank 11

Z

Zappos 78

Image credits

pp v(tl, c&r), vi(l&r), 11–13, 15, 18, 22–26, 28–9, 31–34, 38–39, 56, 59(l), 68(t), 76–77, 80(t), 88, 89(l), 91, 95, 96, 124–7, 130, 136, 140, 144, 148, 173 Cushman & Wakefield; p v(bl) Richard Pickering; p vi(c) Mychael Lyudin (C&W US); pp 1, 16, 19 Huckletree; p 2, 37, 51–2 Heatherwick Studio; pp 4–5, 166 V7; p 7, 42(t&br), 43–44, HMRC; p 45 European Union Mobility Atlas 2021 (EUMA2021) – Mobility of Women, picture: Heinrich-Böll-Stiftung licence: CC-BY-SA 4.0; pp 21, 72–3, 156, 157(b), 162(l) Jack Hobhouse; p 27 Remit Consulting; pp 47–50 HOK; p 53(t) AB Rodgers; p 53(b) Nigel Young/Foster + Partners; pp 55, 61–2 Darren Carter; p 57 United Nations: https://www.un.org/sustainabledevelopment/. The content of this publication has not been approved by the United Nations and does not reflect the views of the United Nations or its officials or Member States; p 59(r) Urban Mind; p 60 The FORE Partnership; p 63 McGregor Coxall; p 64 SDG House, Amsterdam; p 65 James Fairclough; p 67 HALO; pp 68(b), 69–70 BCG; pp 75, 85 Hines, CGIs by Walk The Room; p 80(b) Joseph Pine II & James Gilmore – As in The Experience Economy; p 81 Virgin Money; p 84 Little Houses Group; pp 87, p 93(b) WilkinsonEyre; p 90 Experian; p 93(t) Unsplash/Andres Garcia; p 94 Brendan Bell; p 97 Unsplash/Chuck Givens; pp 99, 113–15 CapitaLand;

pp 101 Brent Cross Town; p 102 Argent/John Sturrock; pp 103–05 ESB; pp 107–09 Aecom; pp 110, 111(c&b) Diageo; p 111(t) Laurence Winram; p 112 Selfie Factory; pp 116–17, 155 Derwent London; pp 119, 164 Mediaserver Hamburg/Andreas Vallbracht; p 120(l) Erica Guilane-Nachez/Adobe Stock; p 120(r) Archivist/Adobe Stock; p 121 Juulijs/Adobe Stock; p 123 Unsplash/Skull Kat; p 128 DNY3D/Adobe Stock; pp 133, 167(cr) BVN/Sharyn Cairns; p 134 Architectural Press Archive/RIBA Collections; p 135 Unsplash/Victoria Museums; p 138 Google; p 139(l) Supamotion/Adobe Stock; p 139(r) Rick/Adobe Stock; p 143(l) Unsplash/Sladjana Karvounis; p 143(c) Unsplash/Timor Garifov; p 143(r) Unsplash/Karl Callwood; pp 147, 168 BVN/Tom Roe; pp 151, 152(t) Studio Gang; pp 152(b), 153(b), 154(t) Tishman Speyer/Pixelflakes; pp 153(t), 154(c&b) WORKac; p 157(tl&tr) Arup; p 158(t) Jim Stephenson; pp 158(b), 159(t&b) © petewebb.com; p 159(c) Zachary Hyland; p 160(t) Raoyang/Adobe Stock; p 160(b) Studio Bonobo/Adobe Stock; p 161 Brad Pict/Adobe Stock; p 162(r) Jan Kattein Architects; p 163 KCAP; p 165(t) David Soanes/Adobe Stock; p 165(b) hnphotography/Adobe Stock; p 167(l) BVN/Martin Seigner; p 167(tr) BVN/John Gollings; p 169 Pillar Visuals; p 170(t) Faulkner Browns Architects; pp 170(b), 175 Nick Kane; p 171 Hufton + Crow